YUKON

COLOUR OF THE LAND – PHOTOGRAPHY BY RICHARD HARTMIER

YUKON

COLOUR OF THE LAND – PHOTOGRAPHY BY RICHARD HARTMIER

LOST MOOSE

THE YUKON PUBLISHERS

WHITEHORSE 1995

Lost Moose is an imprint of Harbour Publishing
Harbour Publishing
Box 219
Madeira Park, BC
V0N 2H0
www.harbourpublishing.com

To my mother and father, who wanted me to get a real job.
—Richard Hartmier

Design by Mike Rice / Catalyst Communications
Printed in Canada

Harbour Publishing acknowledges financial support from the Government of Canada through the Book Publishing Industry Development Program and the Canada Council for the Arts, and from the Province of British Columbia through the British Columbia Arts Council and the Book Publisher's Tax Credit through the Ministry of Provincial Revenue.

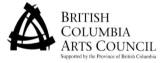

THE CANADA COUNCIL | LE CONSEIL DES ARTS
FOR THE ARTS | DU CANADA
SINCE 1957 | DEPUIS 1957

BRITISH COLUMBIA ARTS COUNCIL
Supported by the Province of British Columbia

Library and Archives Canada Cataloguing in Publication

Hartmier, Richard, 1951–

Yukon : colour of the land / photography by Richard Hartmier.

ISBN 1-55017-331-6

1. Yukon Territory—Pictorial works. I. Title.
FC4012.H37 2005   971.9'103'0222   C2004-907461-X

INTRODUCTION

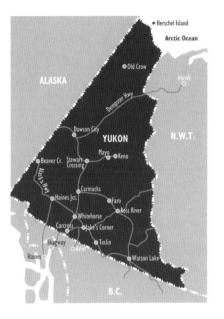

The Yukon is a place to travel endless ribbons of wilderness highway, explore the history of the Klondike Gold Rush or head into the plentiful backcountry.

Irrepressible images are etched into the memories of those who experience this remarkable land. It's the colour of the land, painted by a special kind of light in the north, that creates these vivid impressions.

The colour of the land changes with the hours, days and weeks of the northern summer. It's found in the plants and animals of this majestic and pristine northern wilderness. It's found along mighty rivers, in mountain passes and in hillside meadows lit brilliantly by flowers under a warm summer sun.

Yukon — Colour of the Land is an invitation to share our home as we see it, and as others will remember it. Come and enjoy.

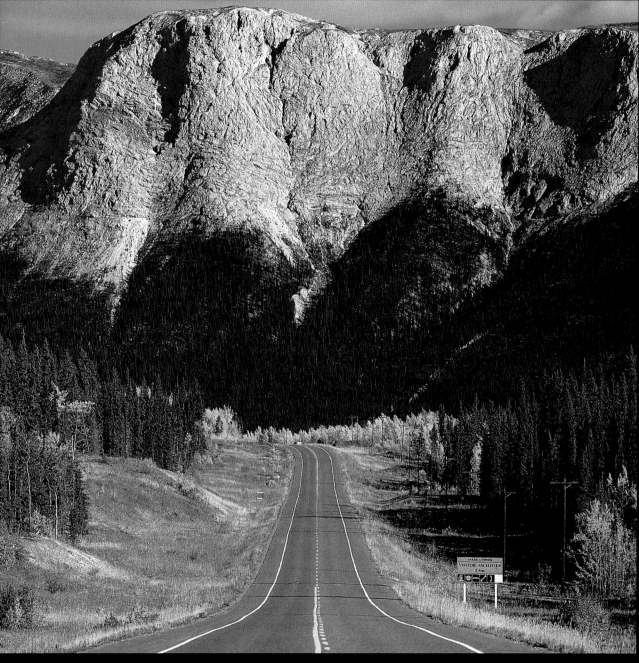

ALASKA HIGHWAY NEAR JAKE'S CORNER

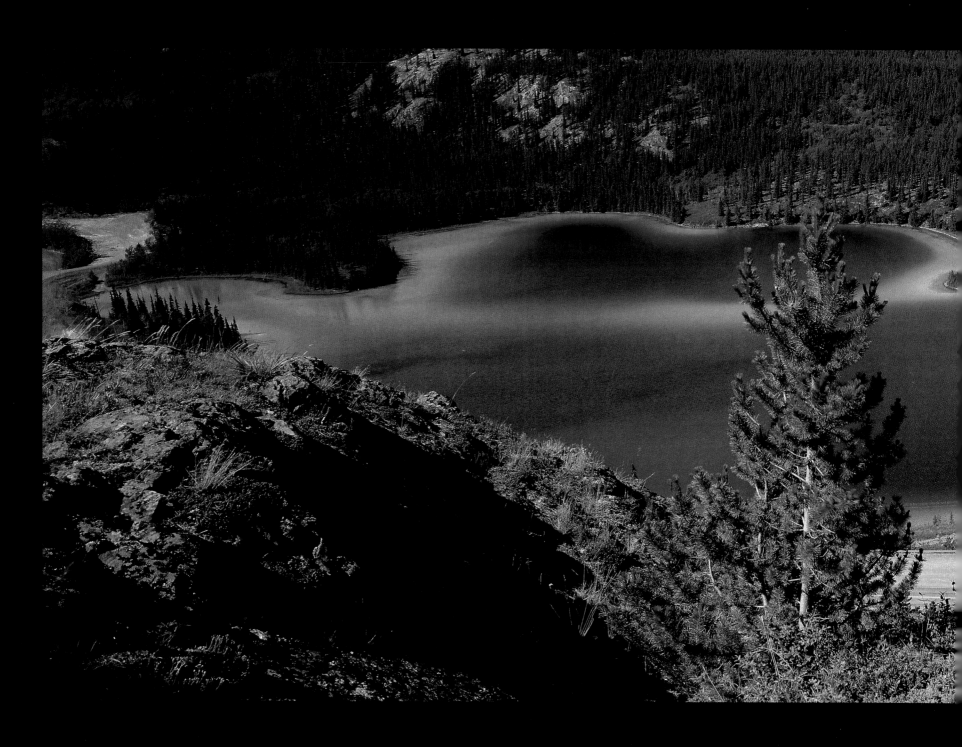

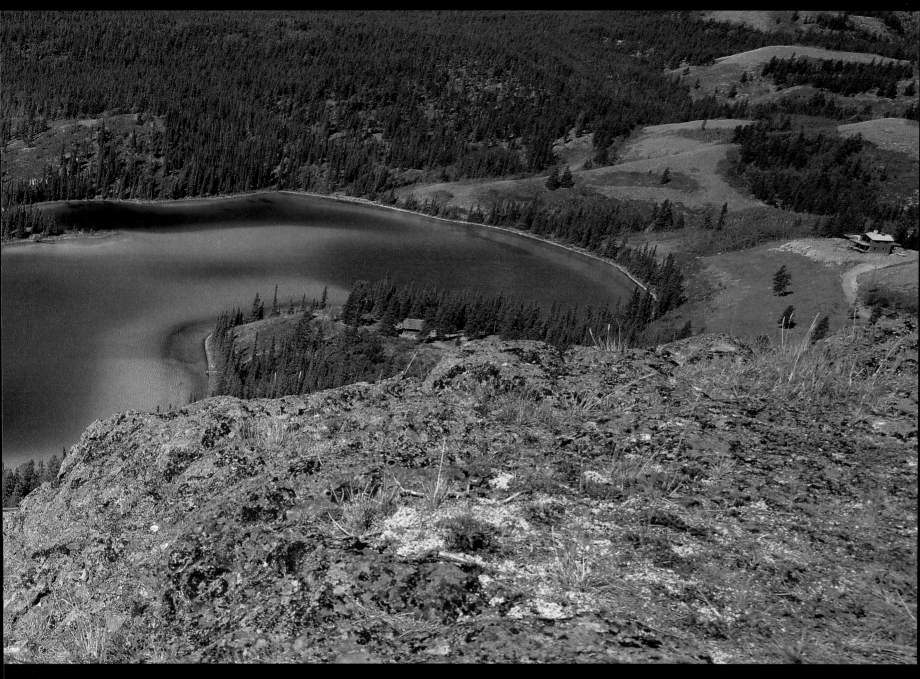

EMERALD LAKE

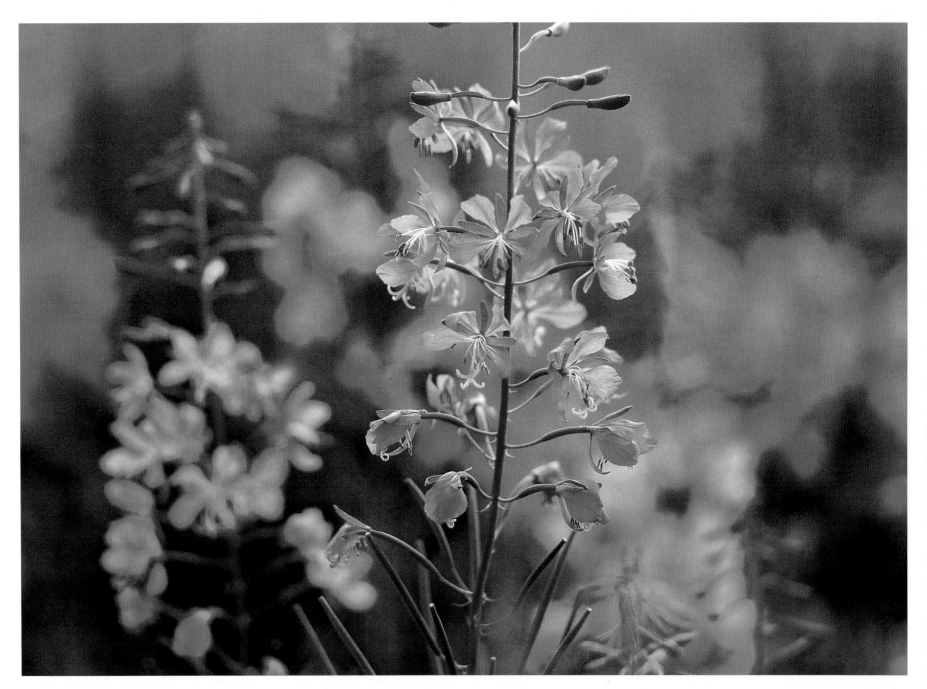

FIREWEED, THE YUKON'S FLORAL EMBLEM

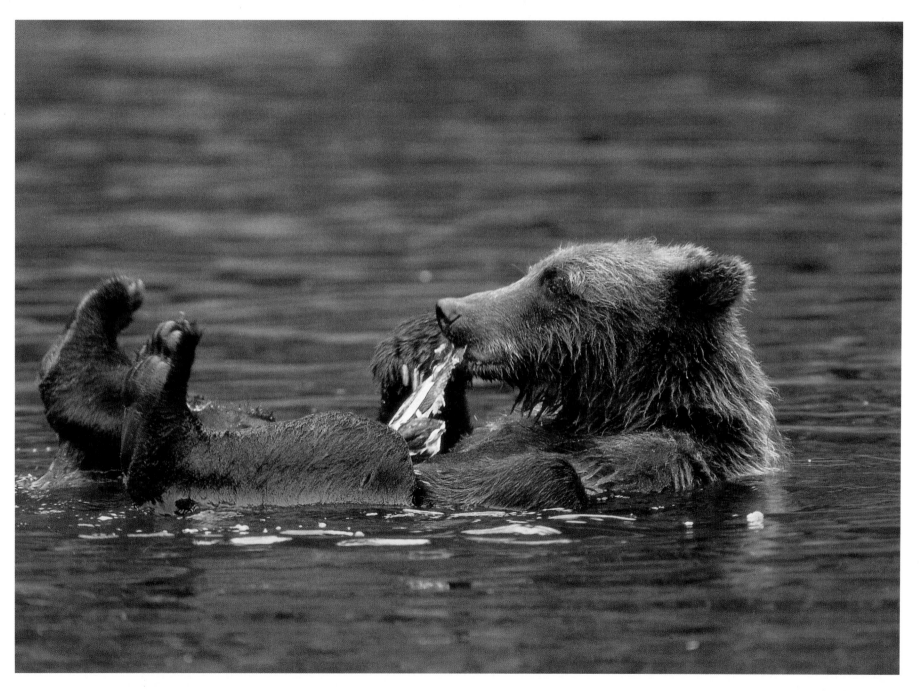

GRIZZLY BEAR

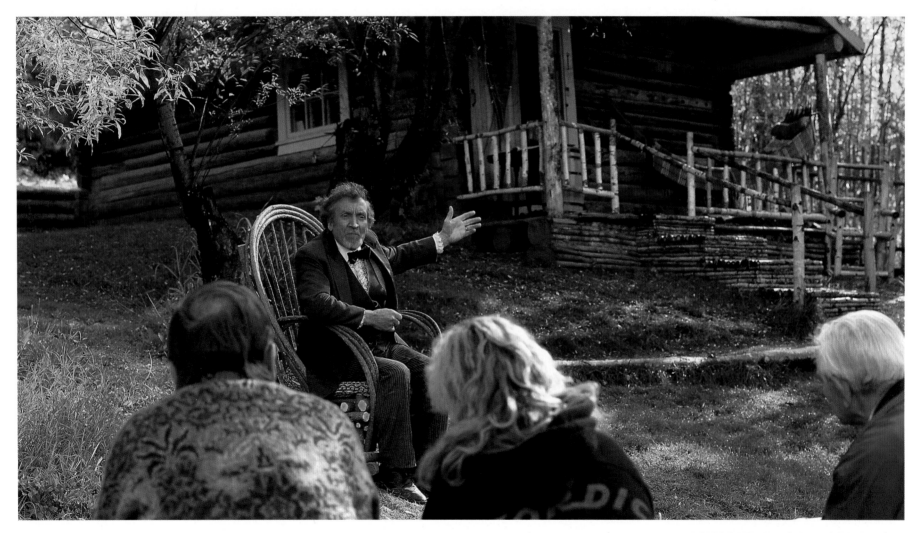

ROBERT SERVICE CABIN, DAWSON CITY

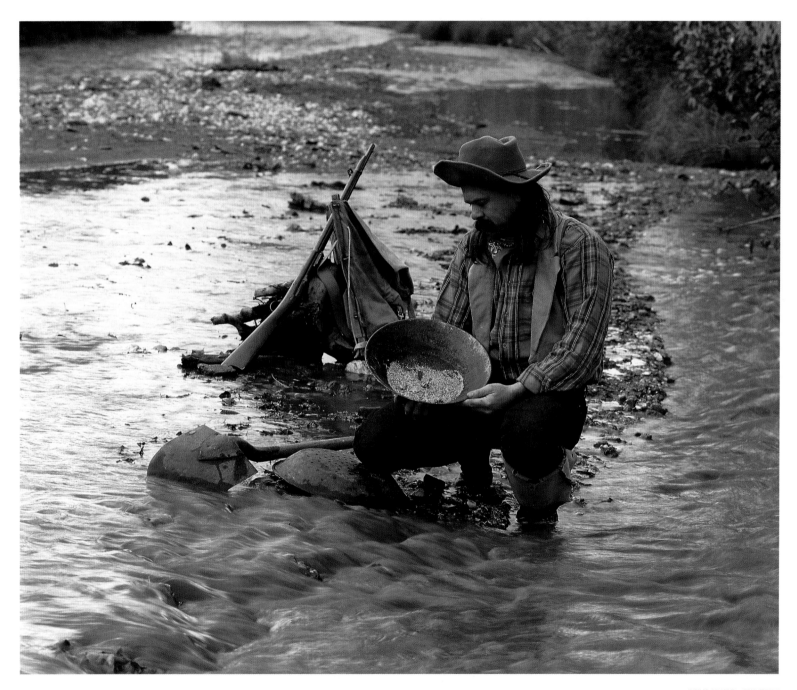

HUNKER CREEK

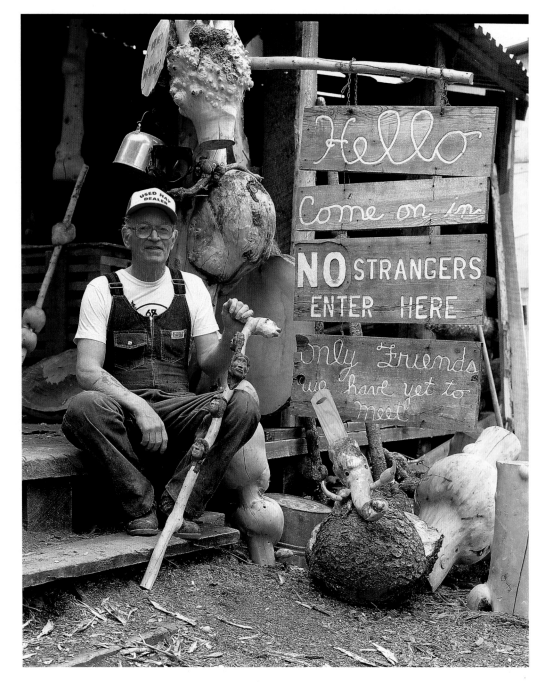

ALASKA HIGHWAY MILE 1118

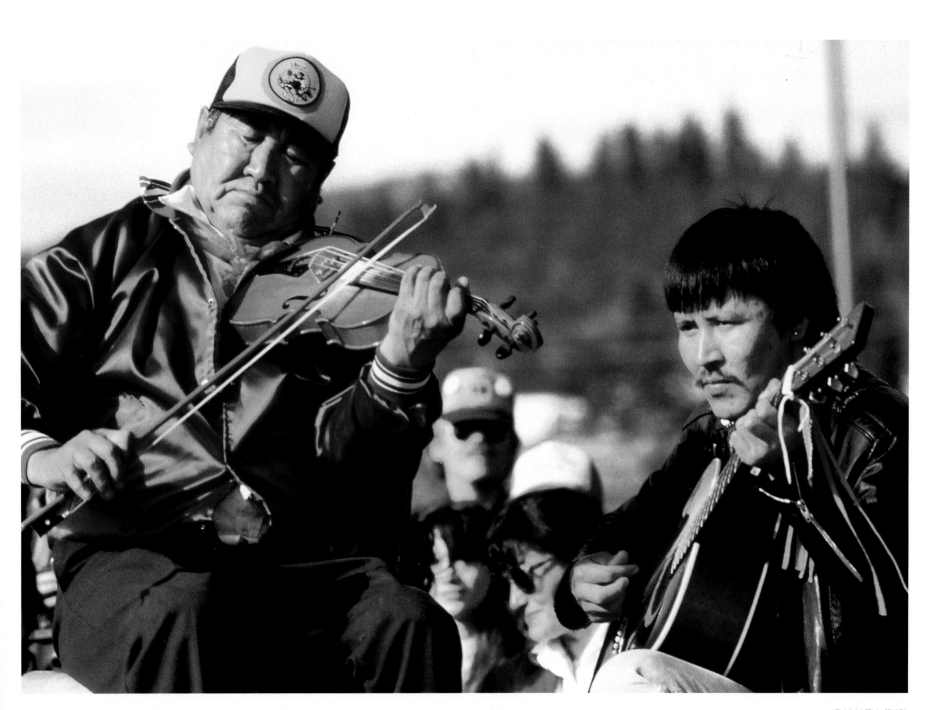

CANADA DAY

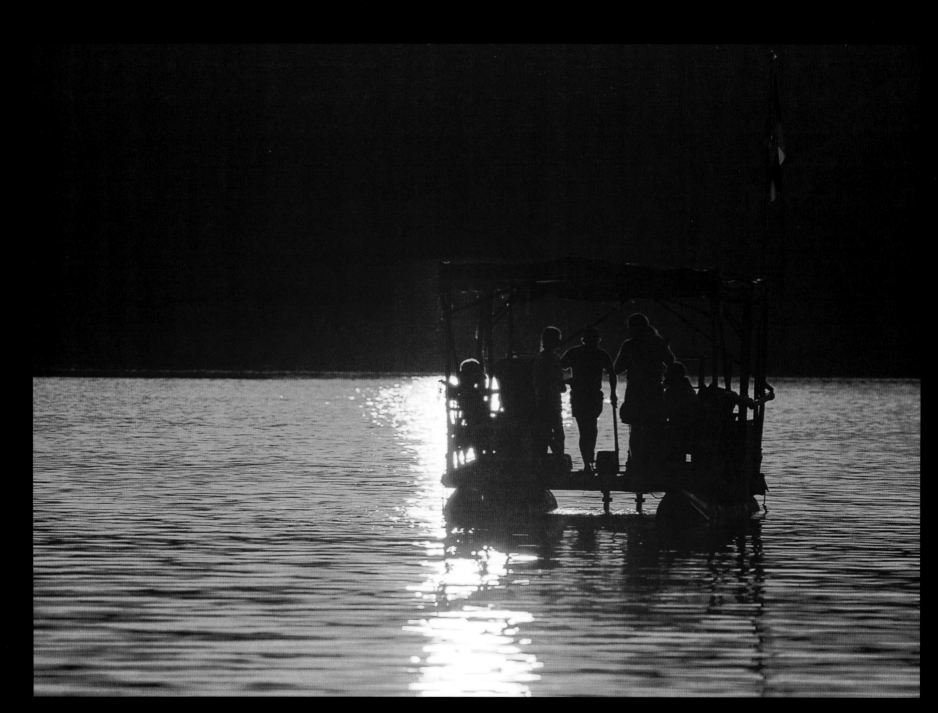

RAFTING THE YUKON RIVER

10 *Dreams*

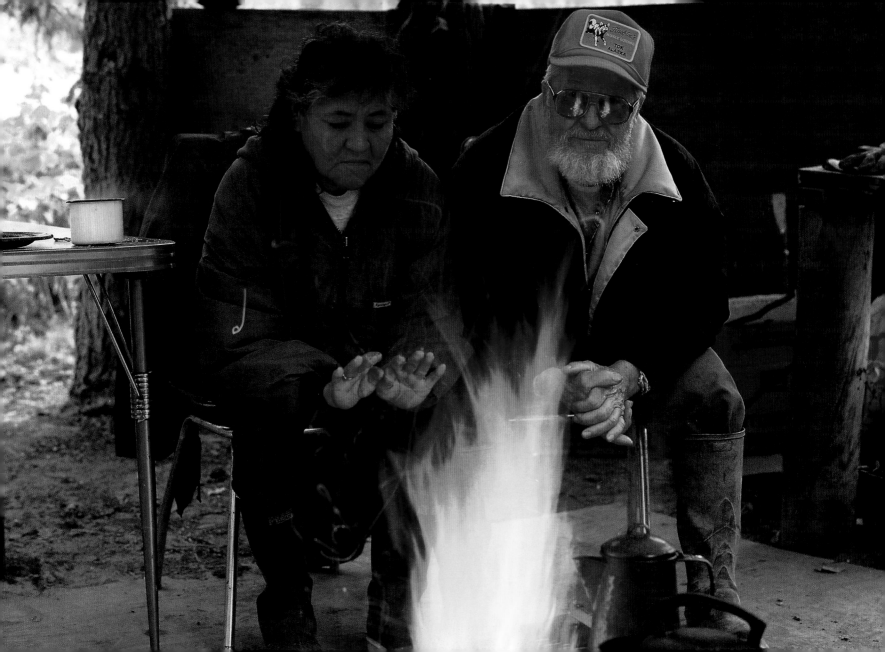

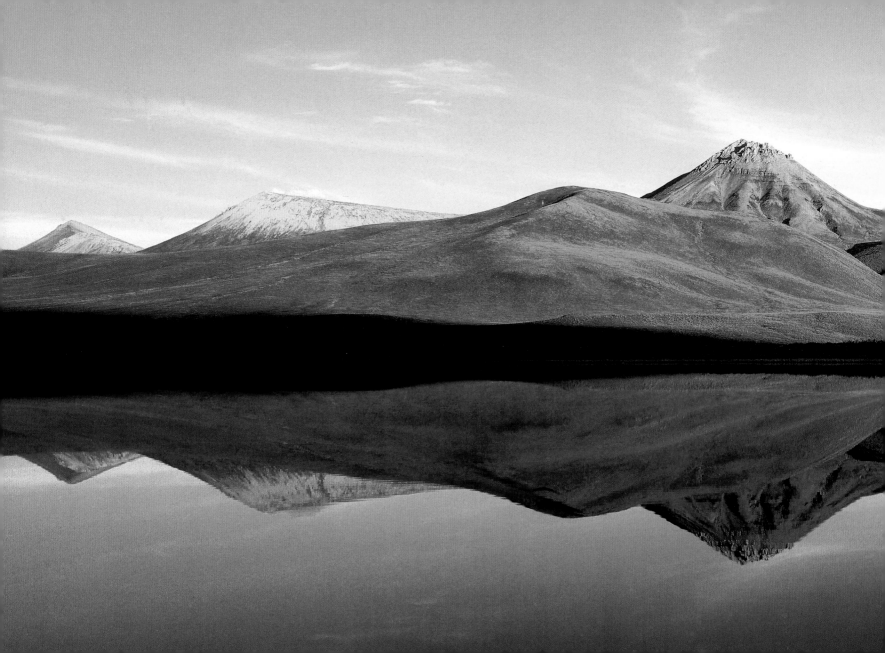

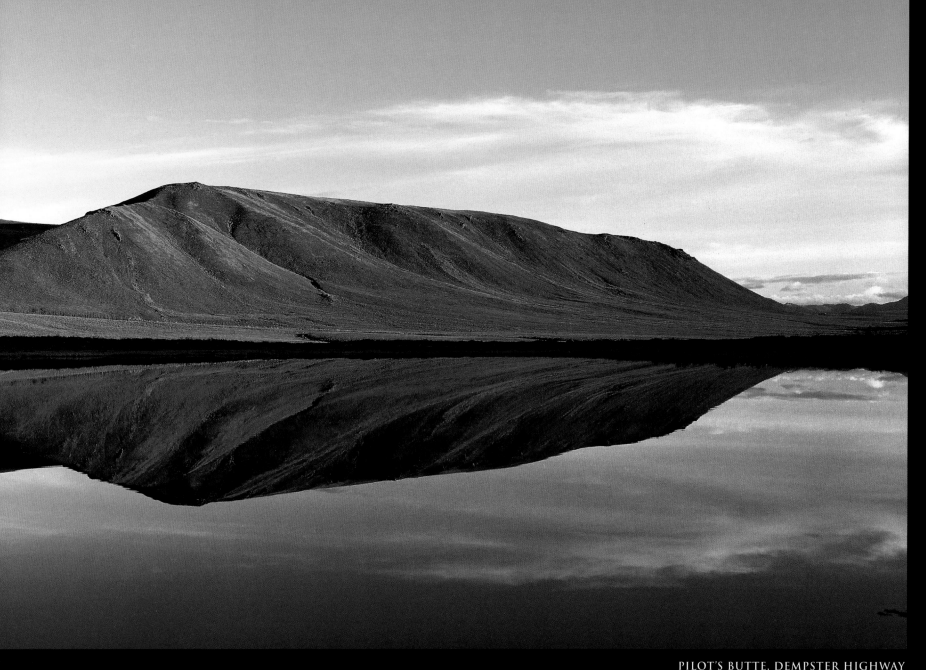

PILOT'S BUTTE, DEMPSTER HIGHWAY

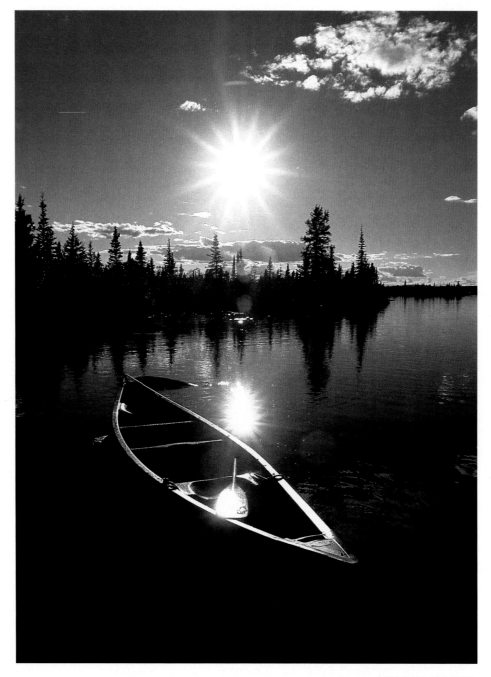

NEAR ROSS RIVER

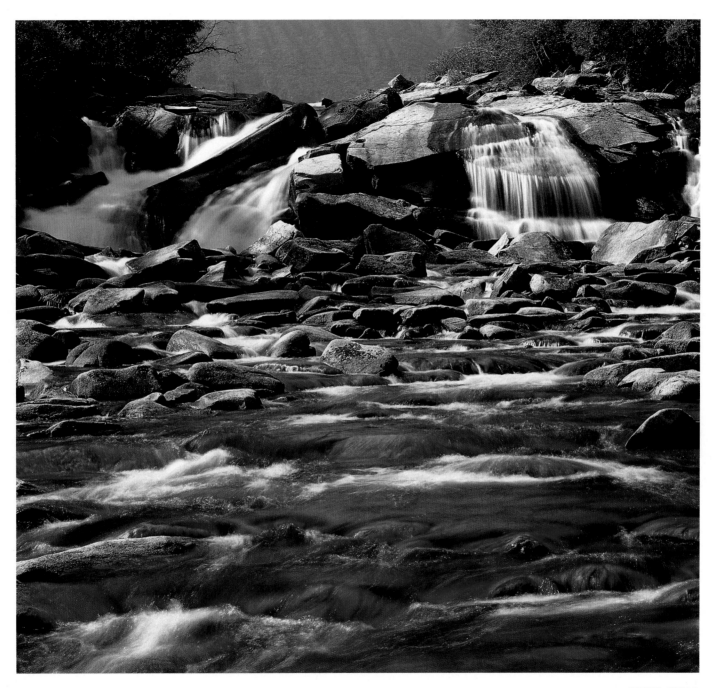

OTTER FALLS

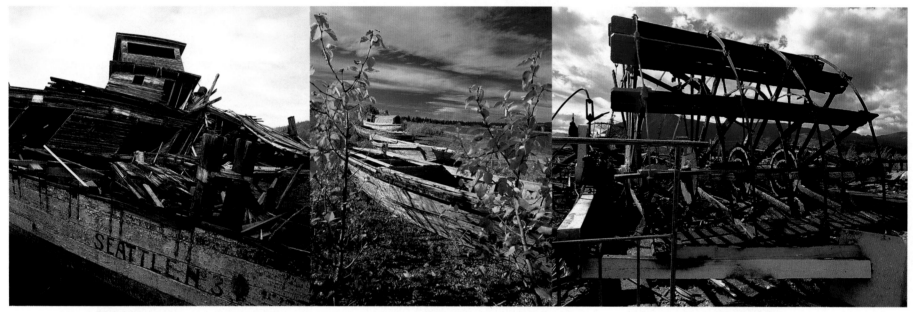

STERNWHEELER GRAVEYARD NEAR DAWSON   BURWASH LANDING   TUTSHI REMAINS AT CARCROSS

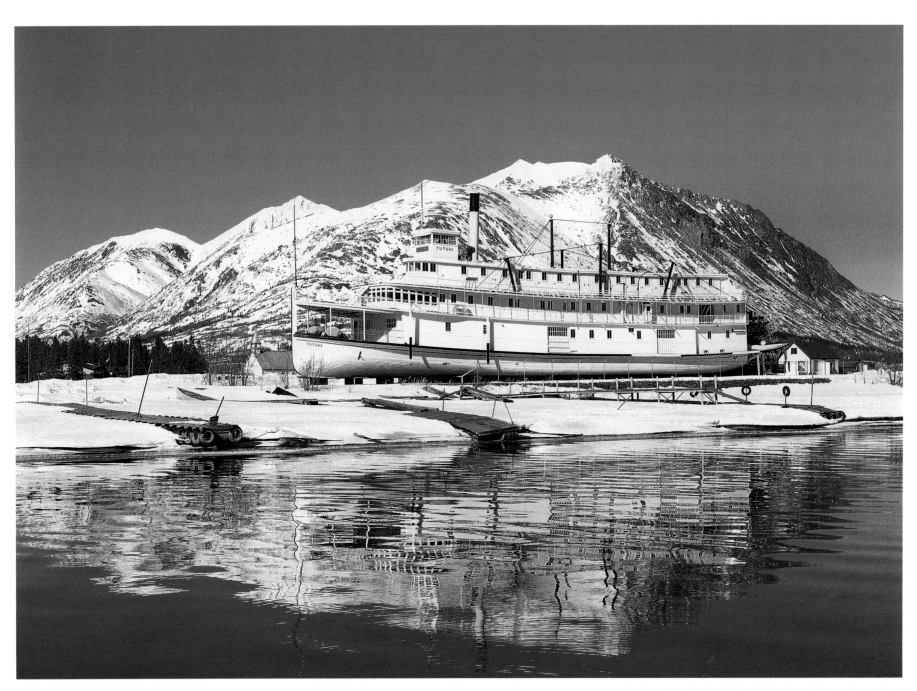

S.S. TUTSHI BEFORE FIRE BURNED IT DOWN

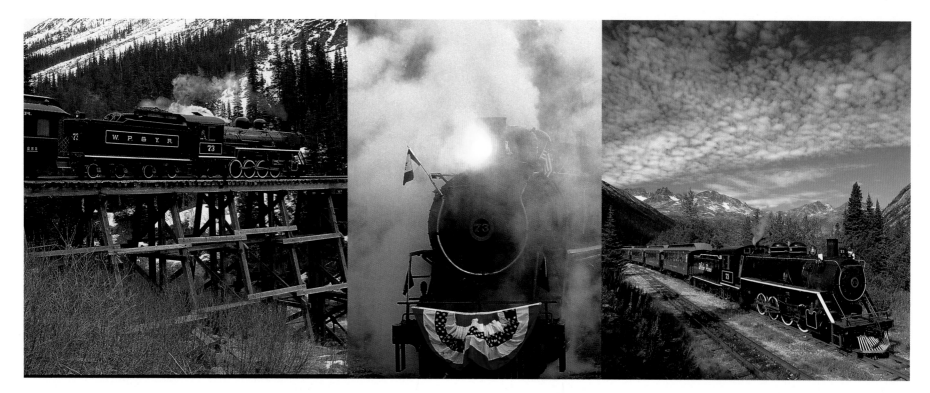

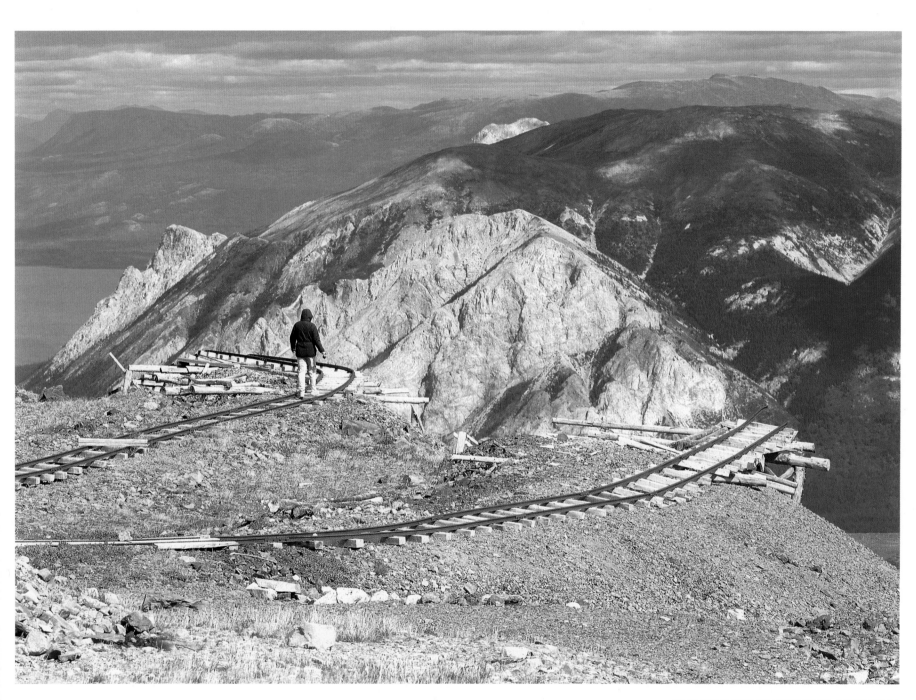

OLD MINE SITE ON MONTANA MOUNTAIN

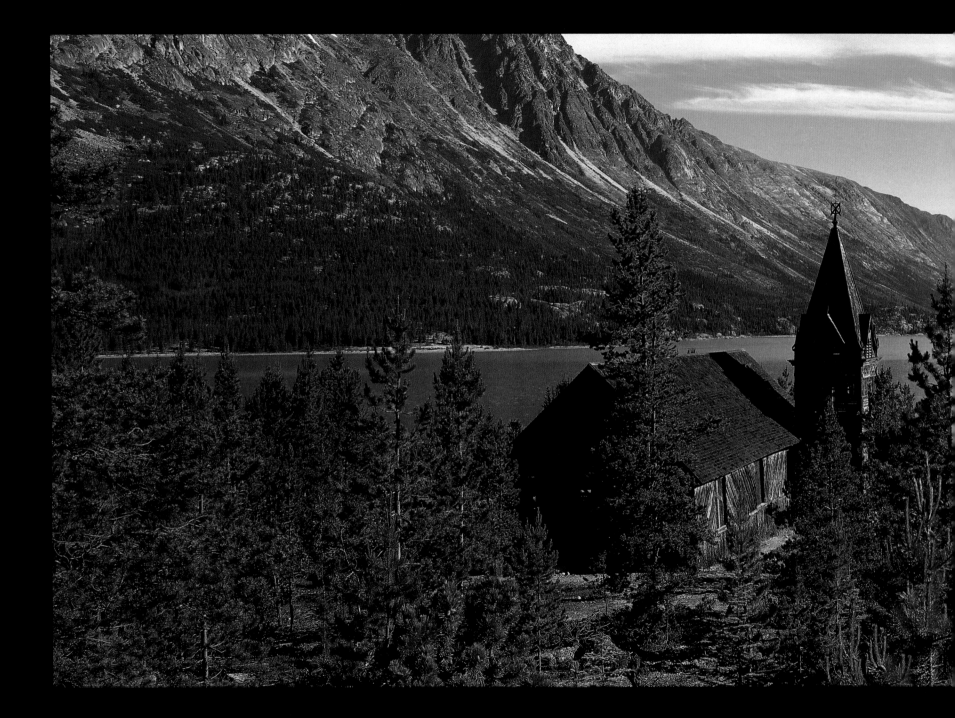

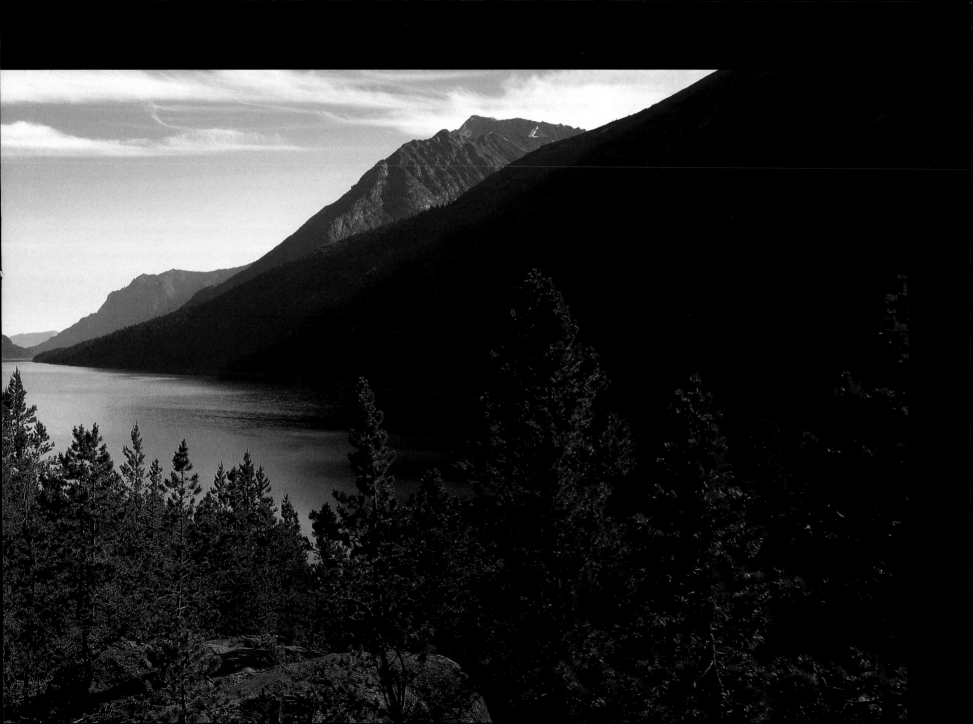

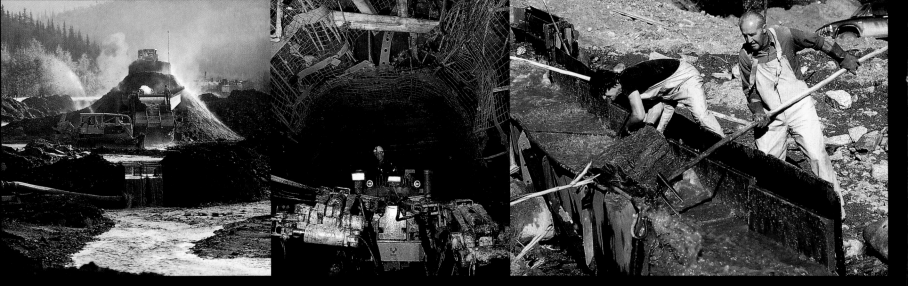

PLACER MINING IN DAWSON   UNDERGROUND AT SA DENA HES MINE   GRANDSON AND GRANDFATHER PLACER MINING NEAR MAYO

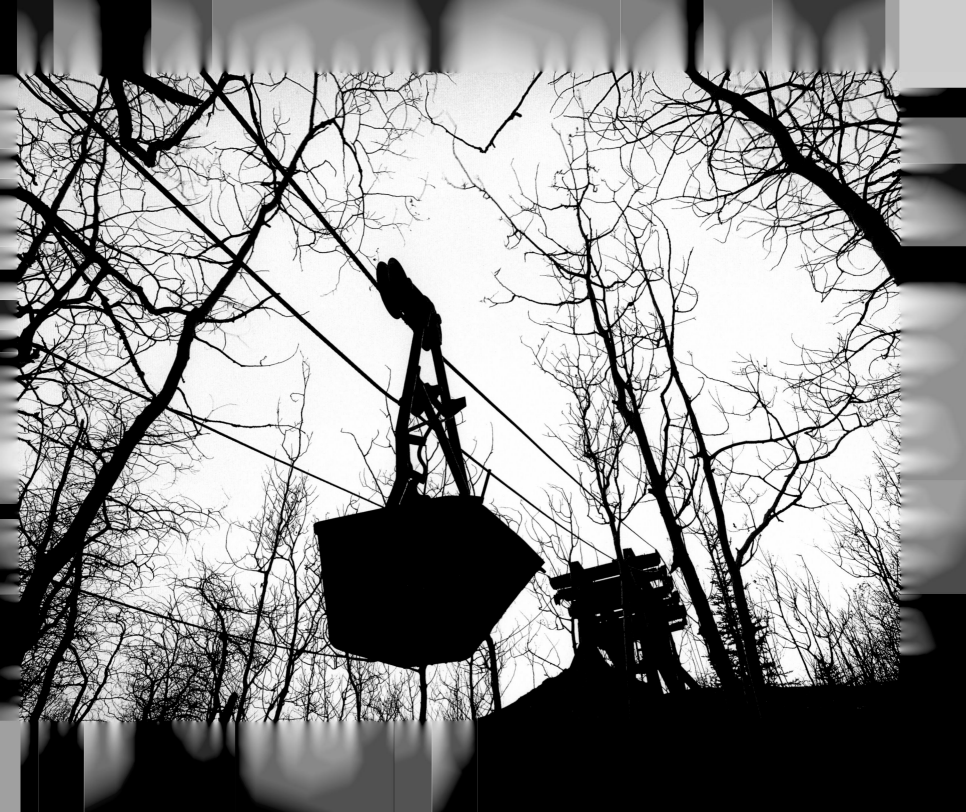

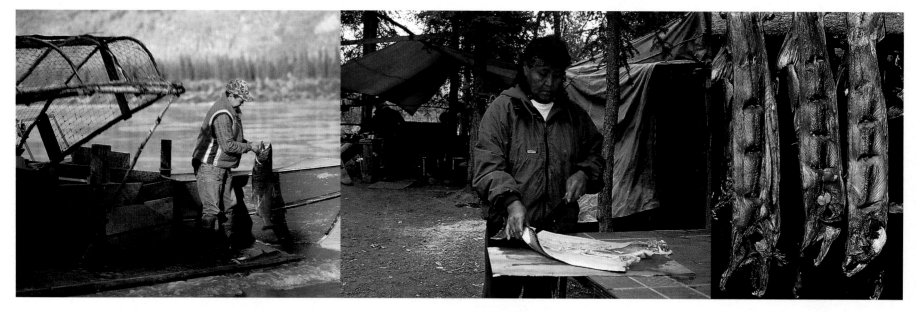

SALMON FISHWHEEL NEAR DAWSON   FISH CAMP – A YUKON TRADITION   FISH DRYING NEAR OLD CROW

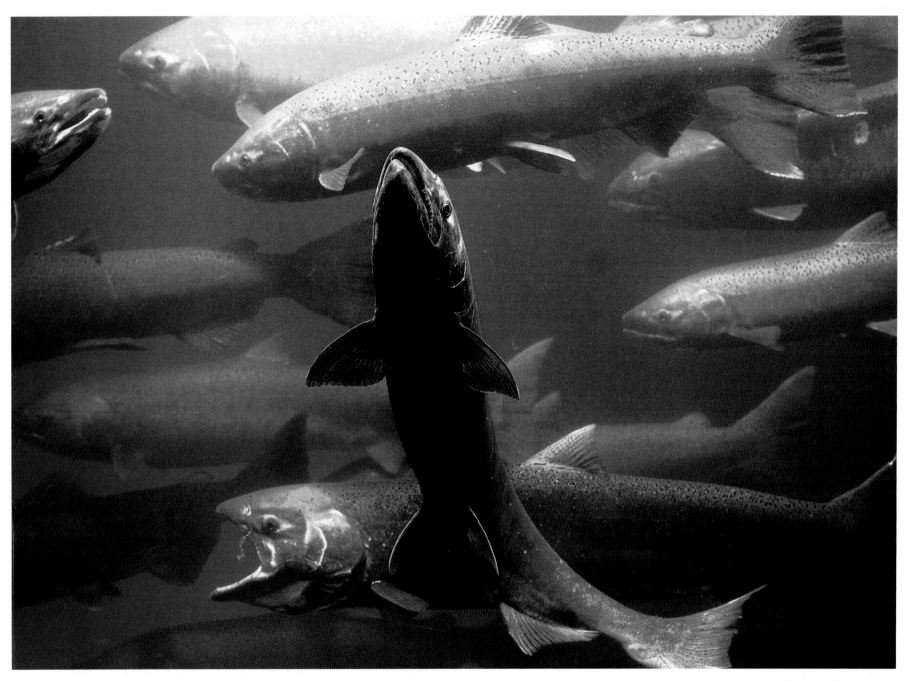

MIGRATING SALMON AT WHITEHORSE FISH LADDER

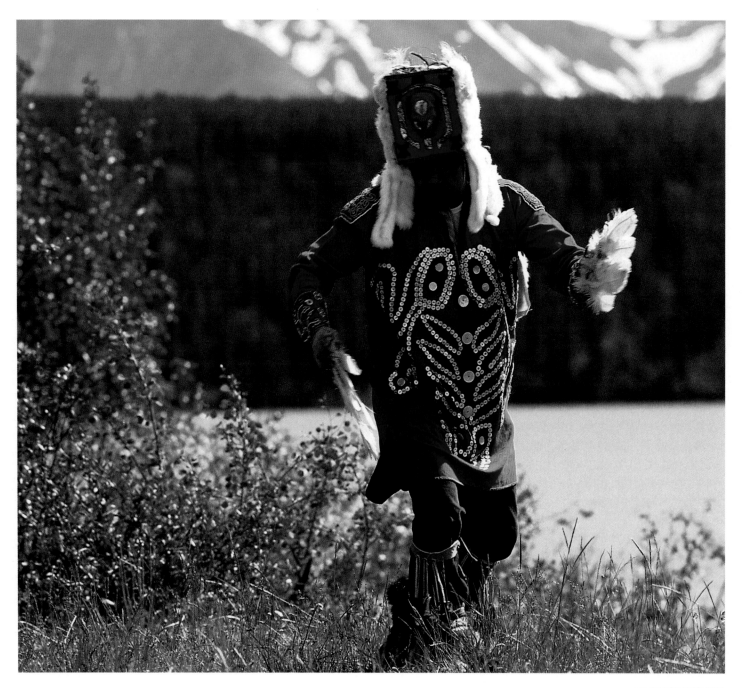

TLINGIT DANCE

Tradition

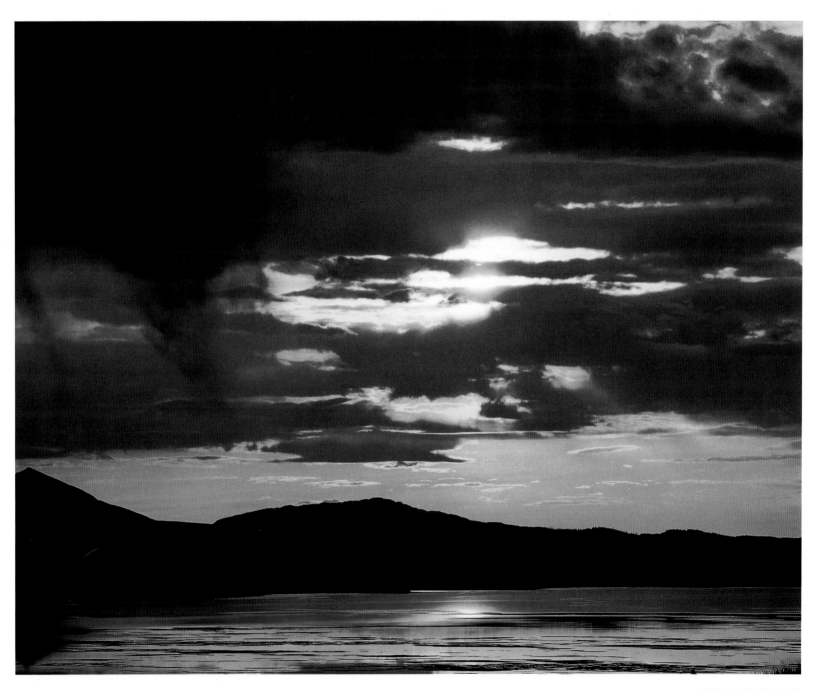

LITTLE ATLIN LAKE

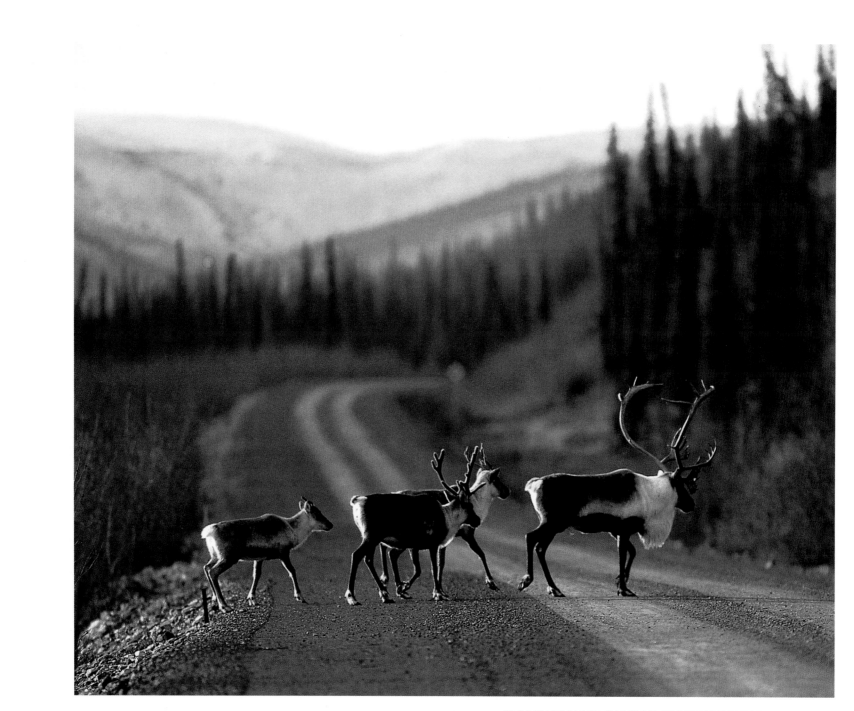

BARRENGROUND CARIBOU CROSSING DEMPSTER HIGHWAY

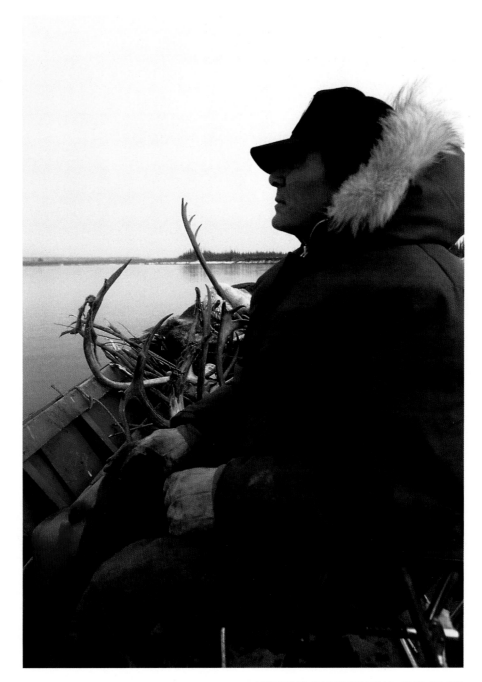

HUNTING CARIBOU NEAR OLD CROW

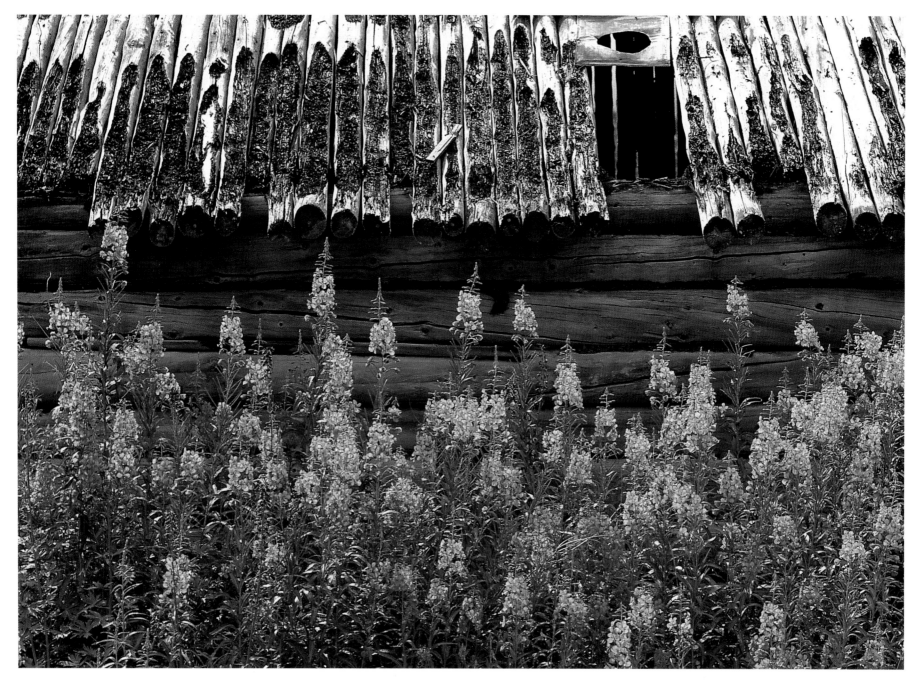

SILVER CITY

30   Neighbourhoods

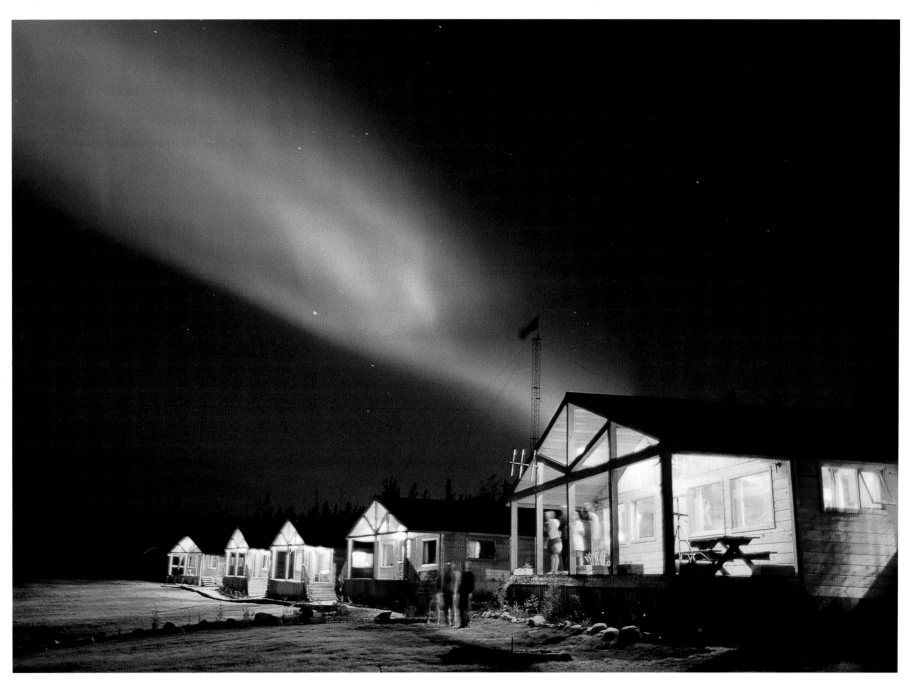

NORTHERN LIGHTS AT A WILDERNESS LODGE

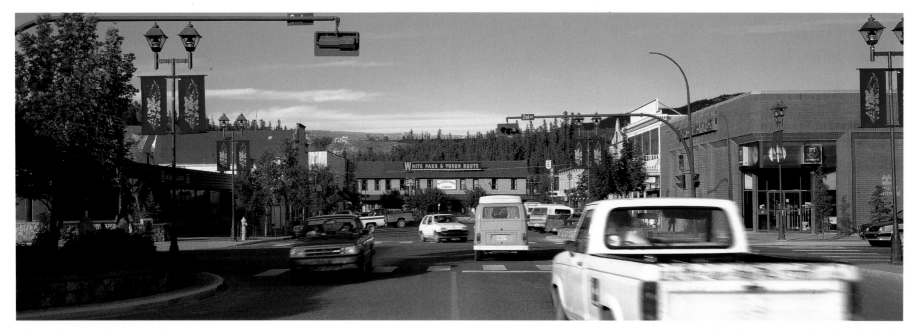

SECOND AND MAIN, WHITEHORSE

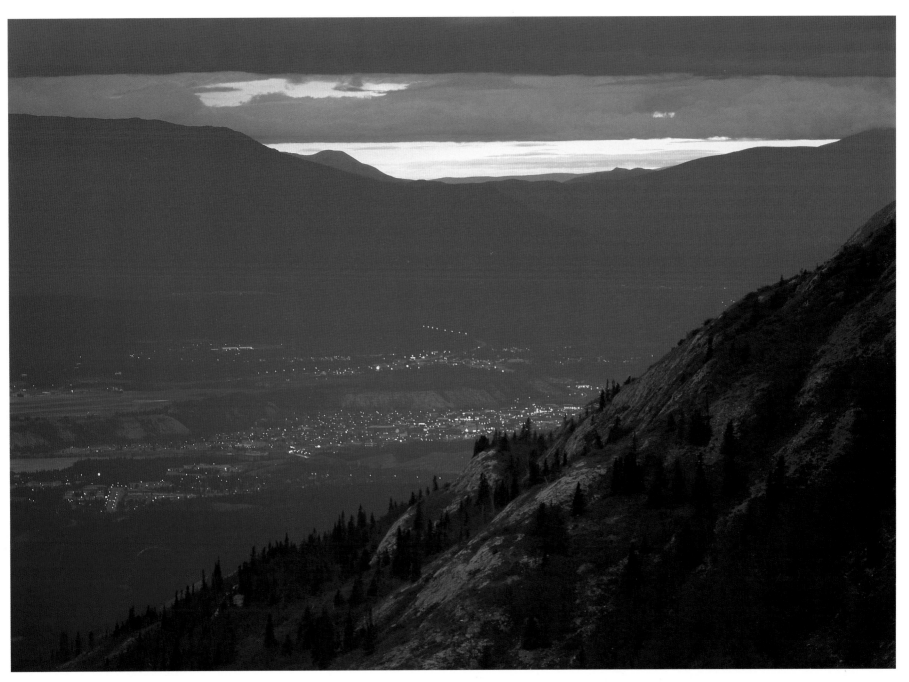

THE YUKON'S CAPITAL, WHITEHORSE, FROM GREY MOUNTAIN

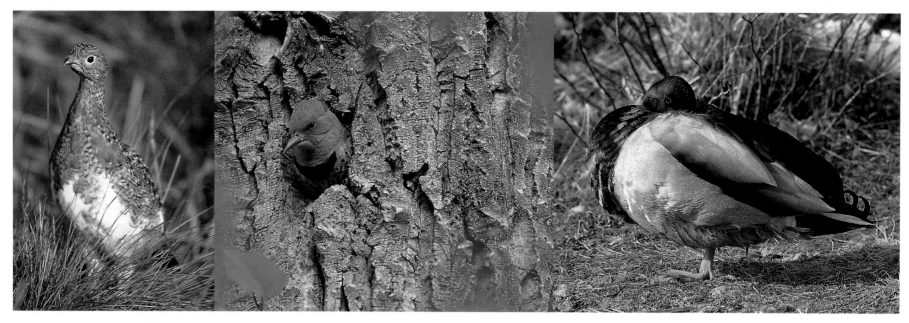

PTARMIGAN   FEMALE NORTHERN FLICKER   MALLARD

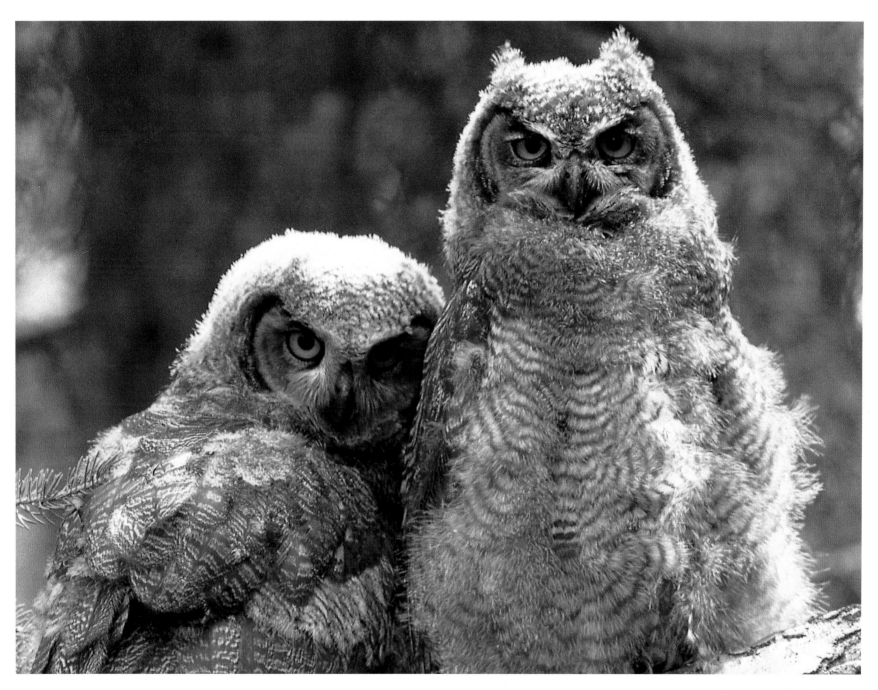

BABY GREAT HORNED OWLS

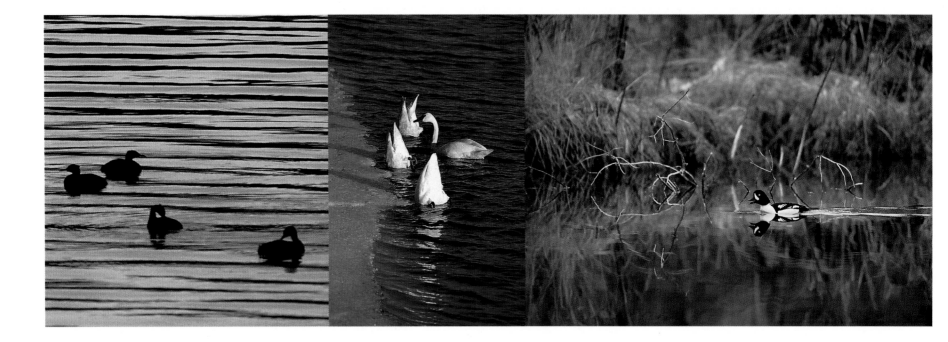

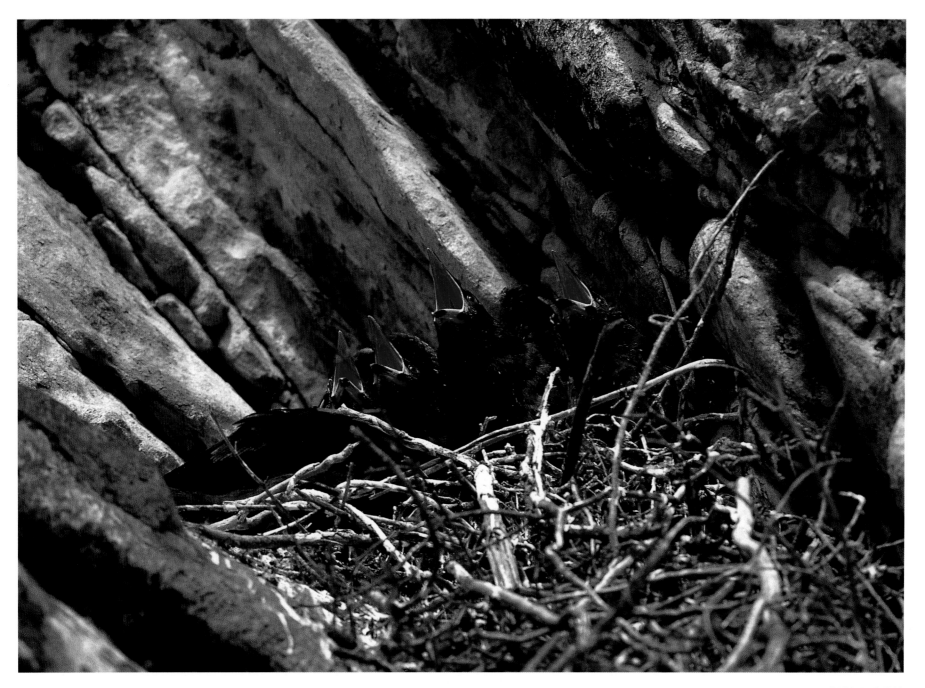

BABY RAVENS

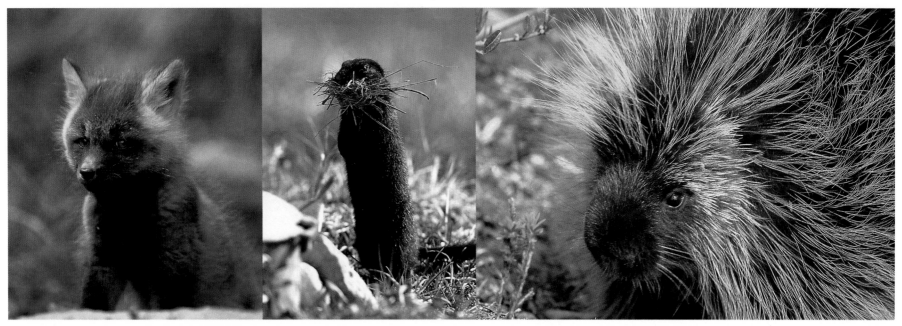

YOUNG FOX   COAL BLACK GROUND SQUIRREL   PORCUPINE

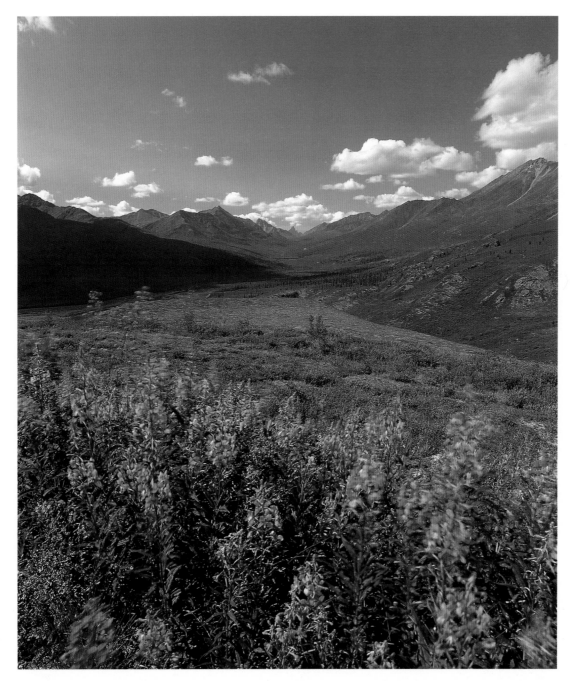

TUNDRA ON THE DEMPSTER, NEAR THE ARCTIC CIRCLE

Colours

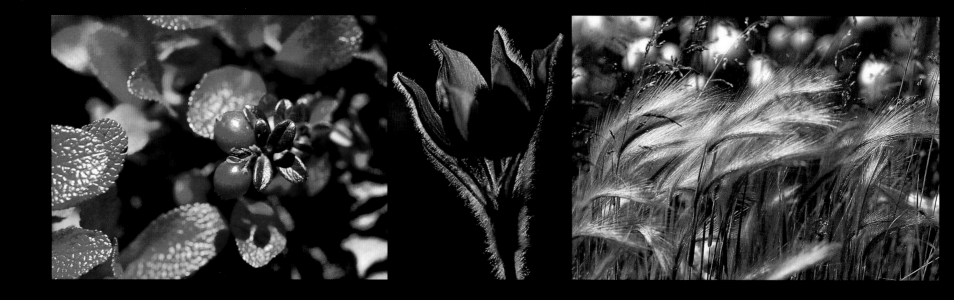

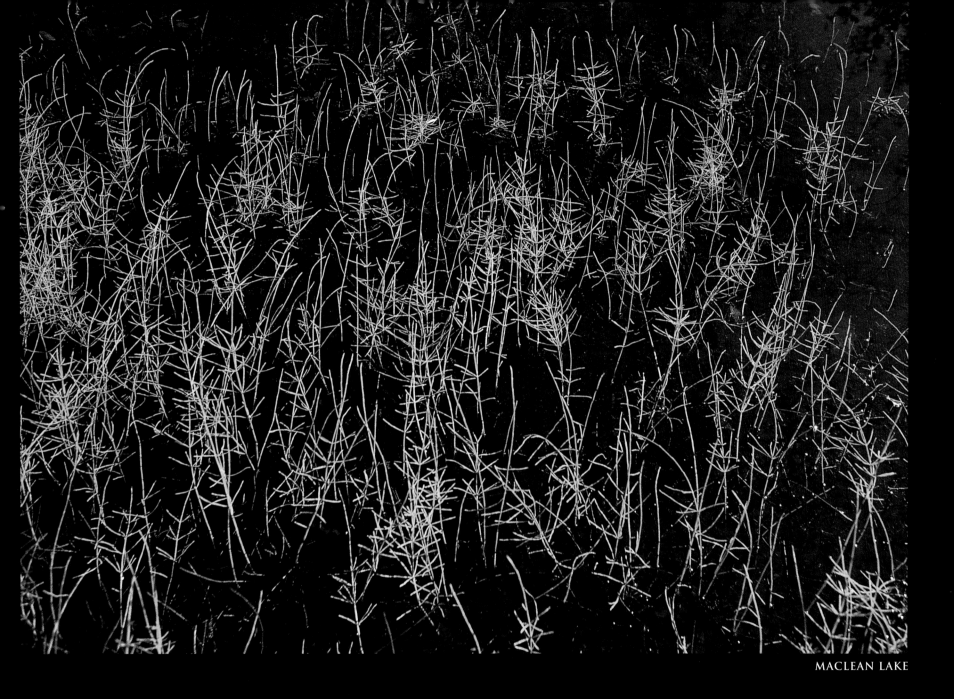

MACLEAN LAKE

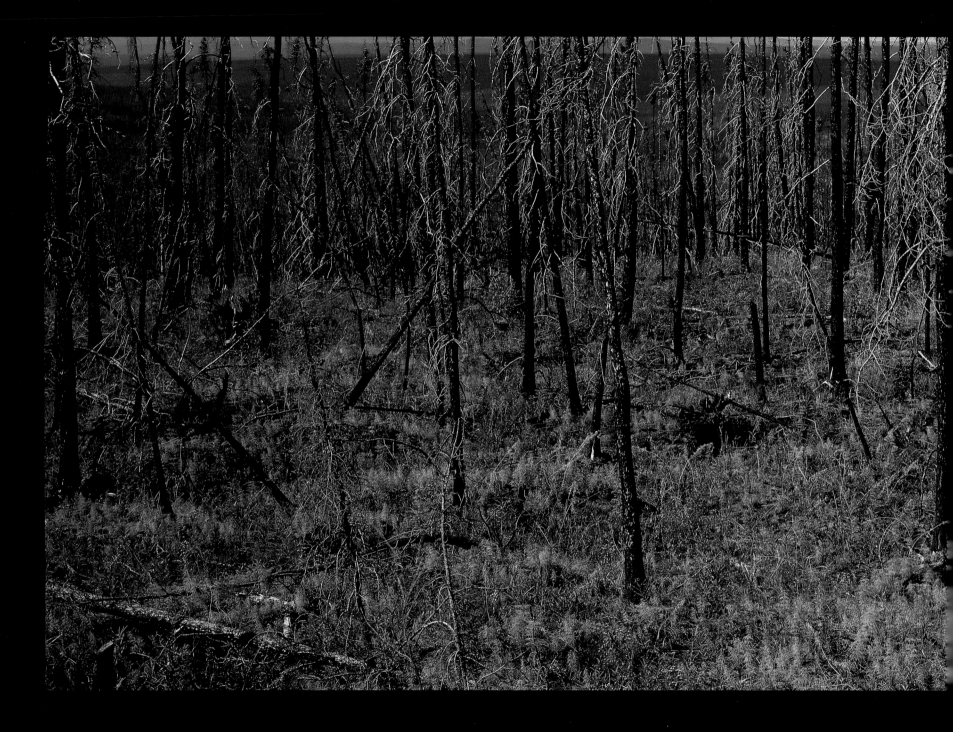

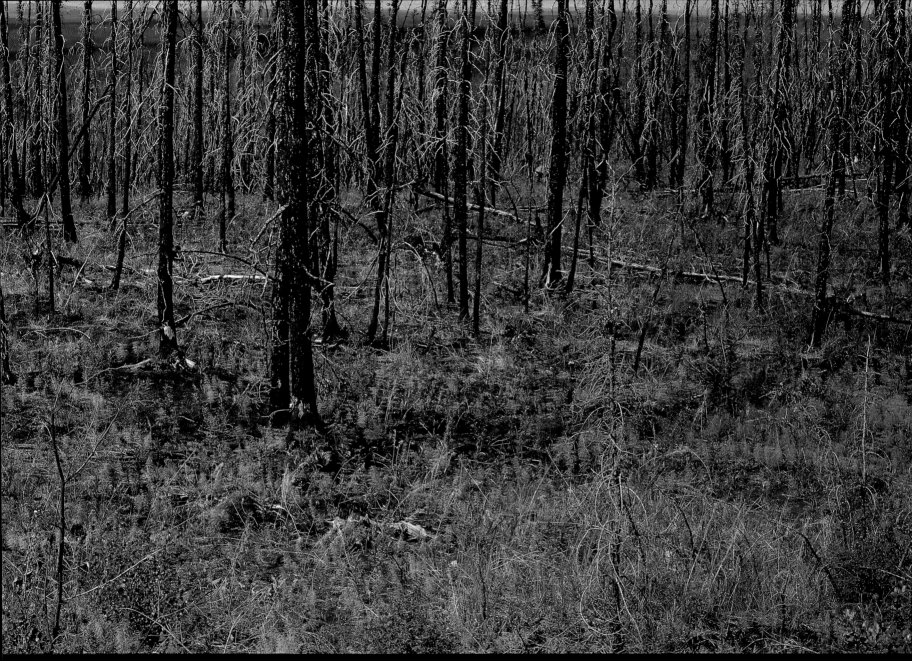

NEW GROWTH EMERGES AFTER A FOREST FIRE ON EAGLE PLAINS

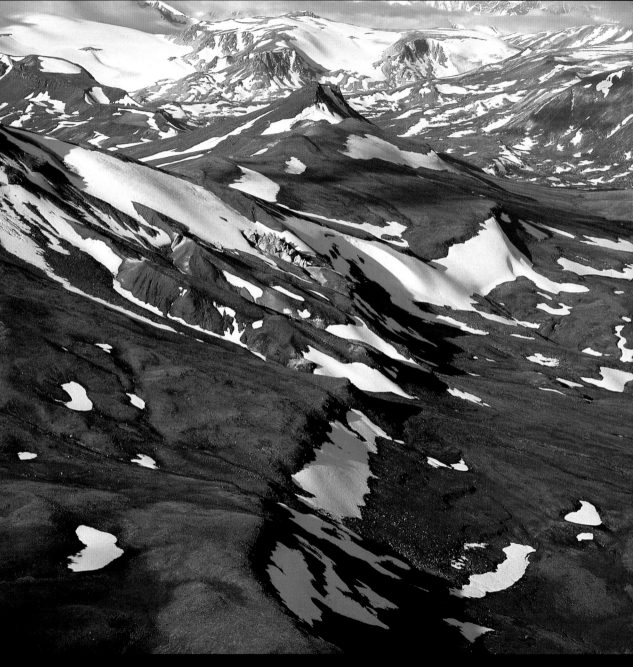

KLUANE PARK

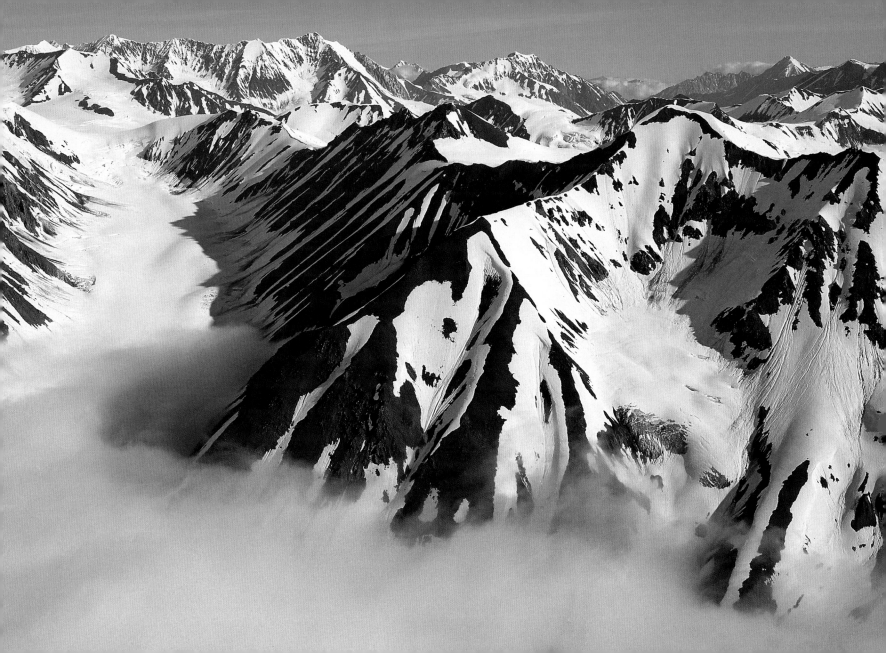

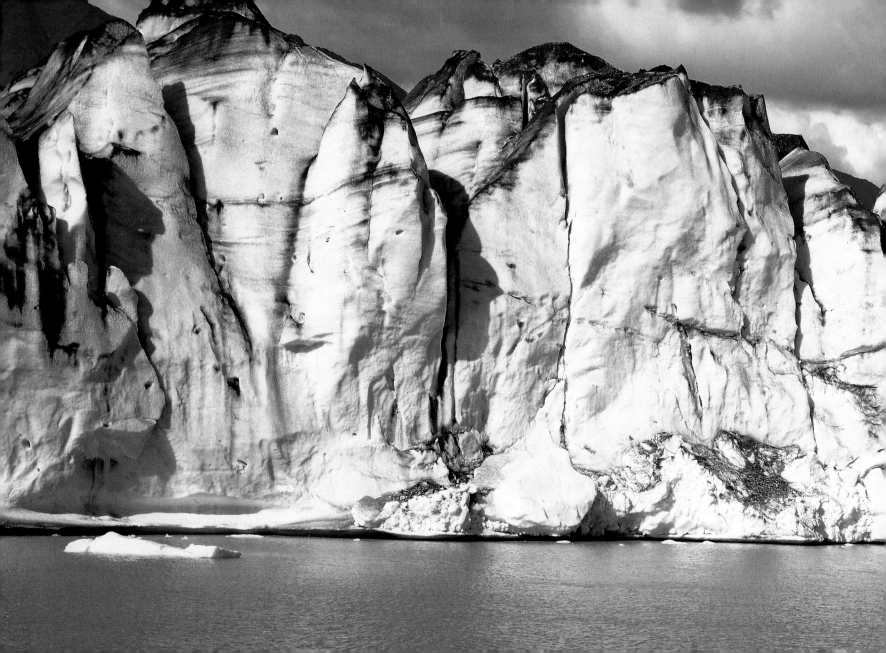

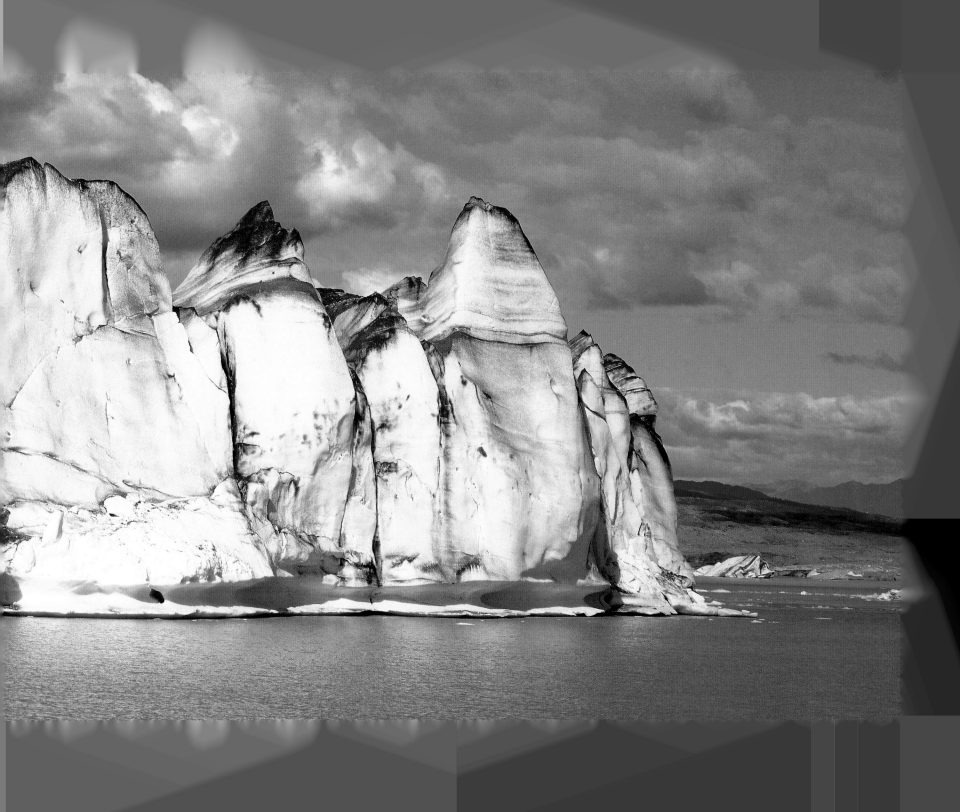

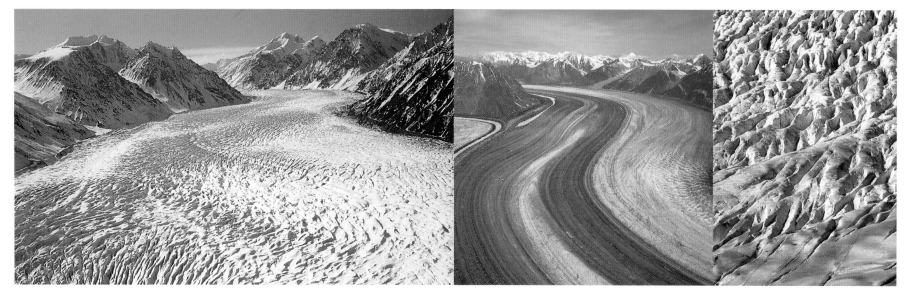

DONJEK GLACIER   KASKAWULSH GLACIER

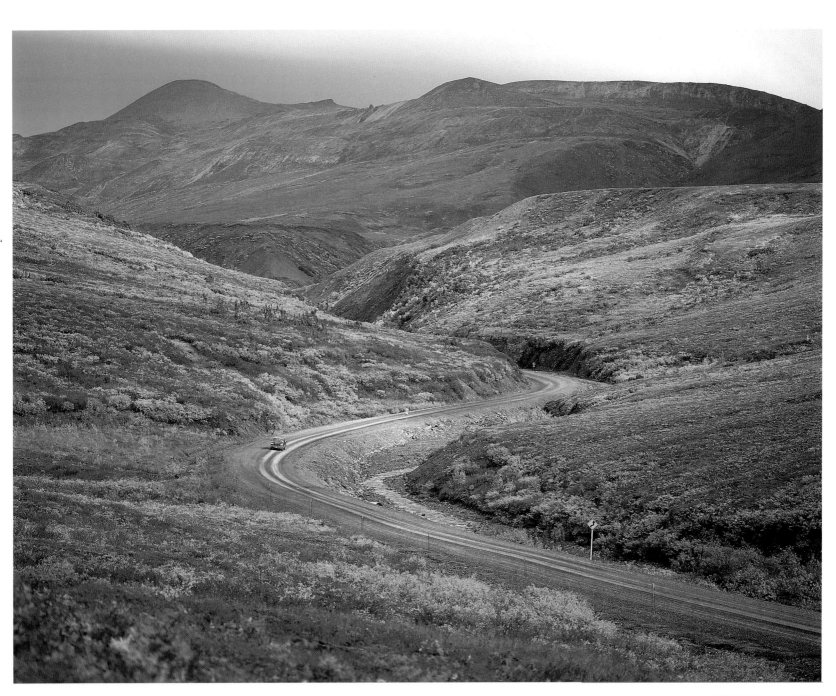

DEMPSTER HIGHWAY

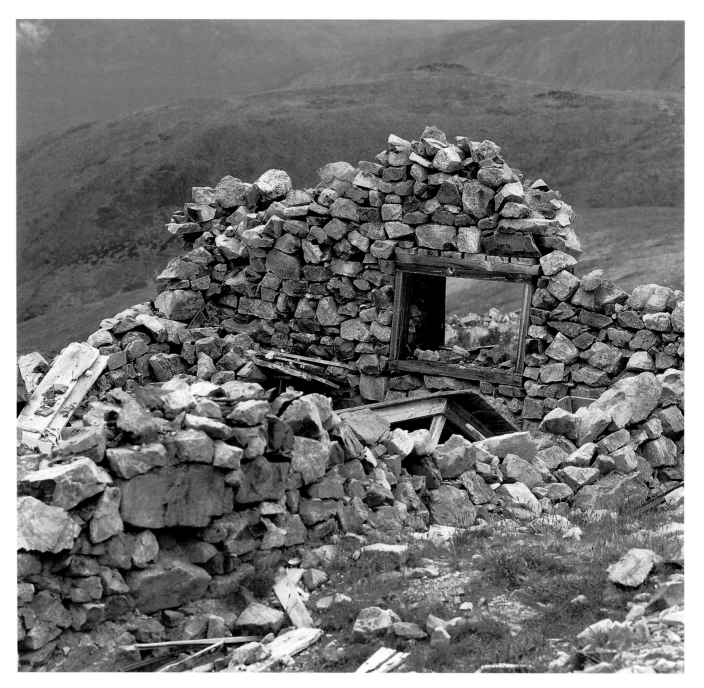

STONE HOUSE, MONTANA MOUNTAIN

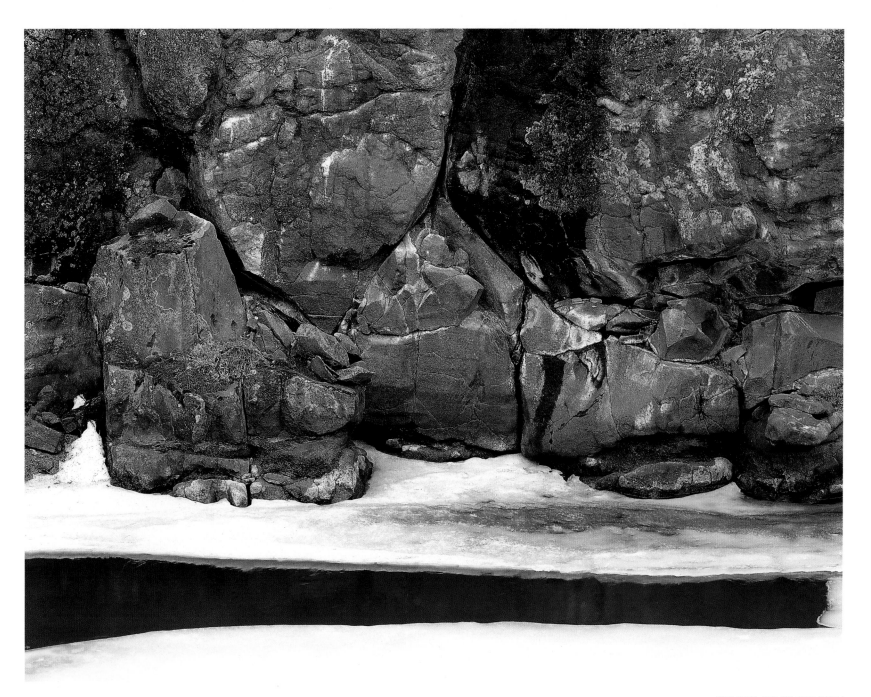

SPRING, MILES CANYON

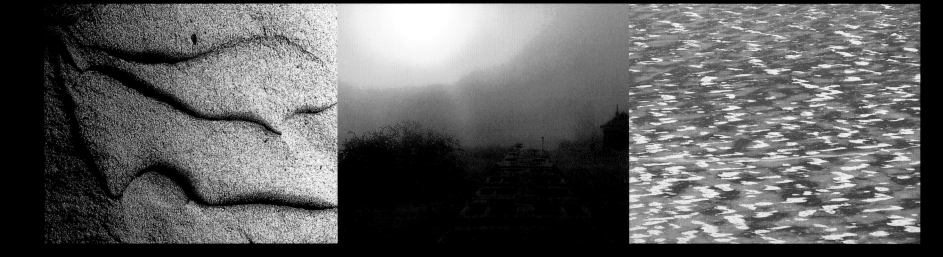

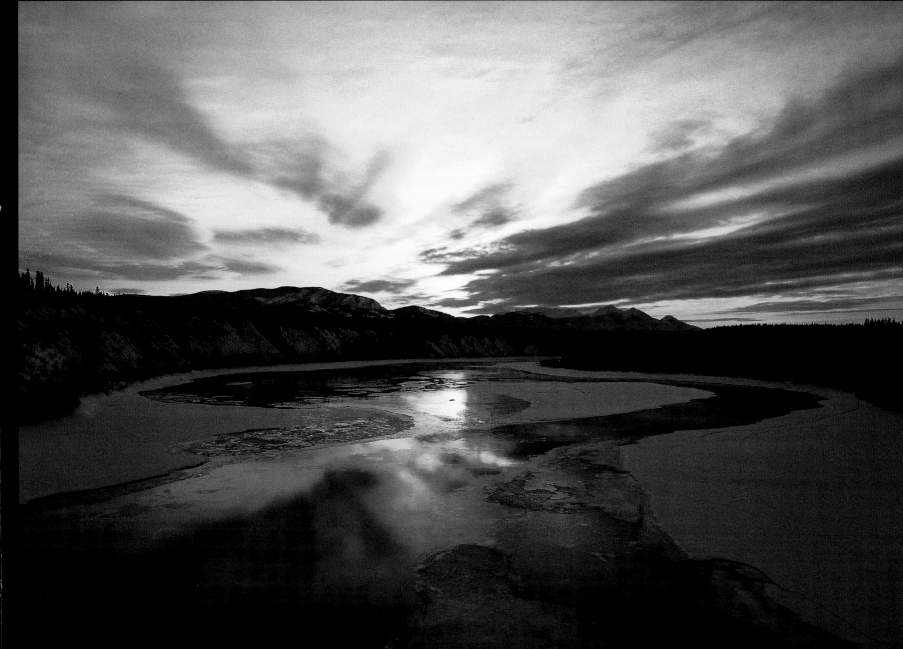

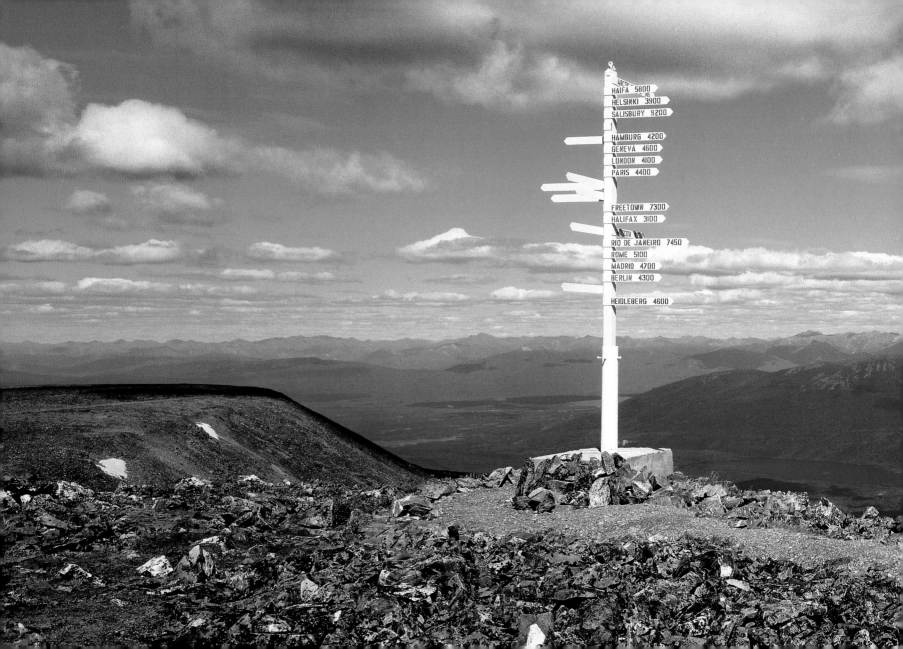

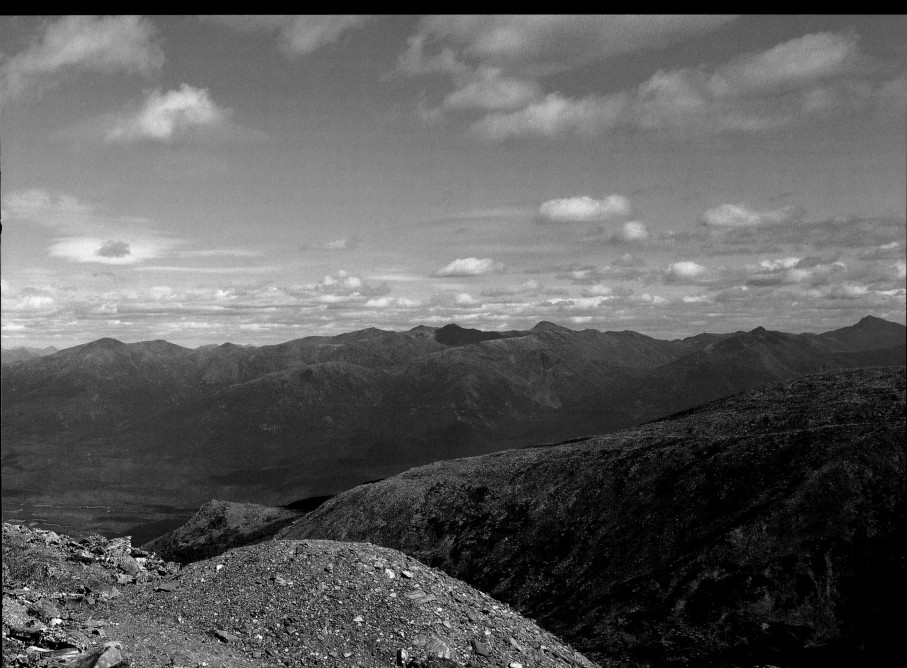

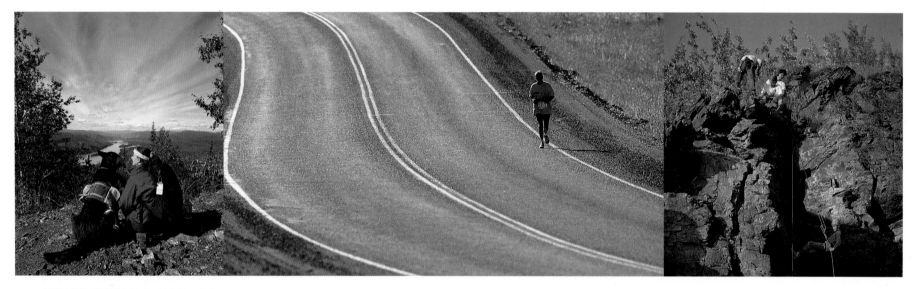

MIDNIGHT DOME, DAWSON CITY · ROAD RELAY RACE, NEAR WHITEHORSE · NEAR DAWSON

A place to enjoy

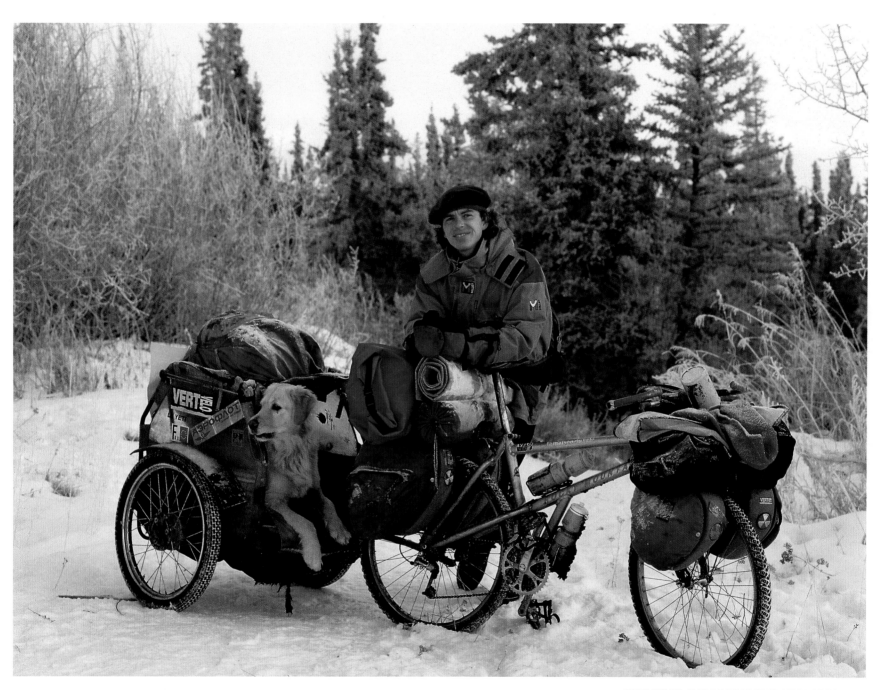

CYCLIST TRAVELLING THE ALASKA HIGHWAY

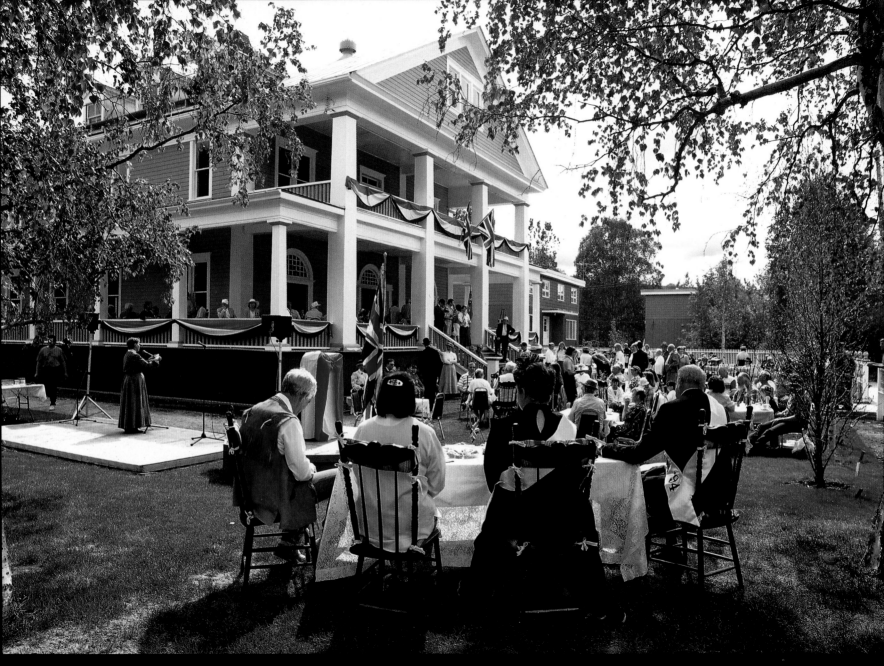

COMMISSIONER'S TEA, DAWSON

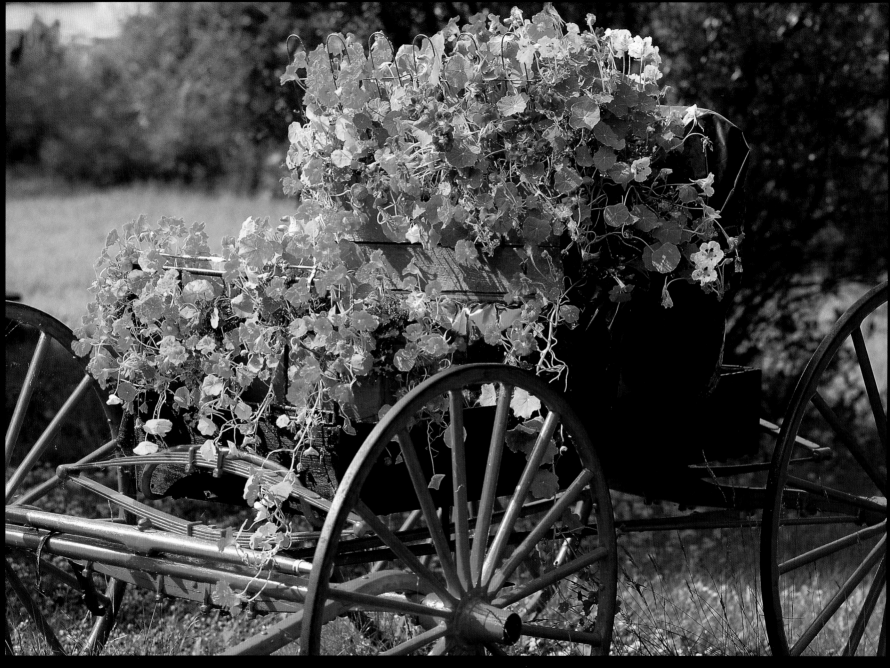

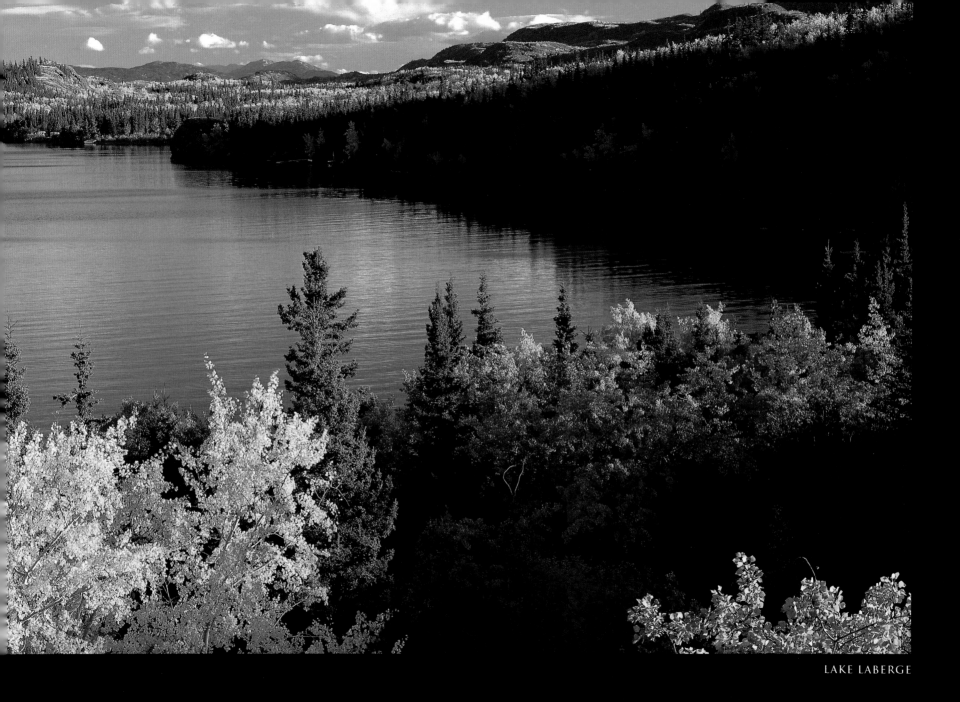

LAKE LABERGE

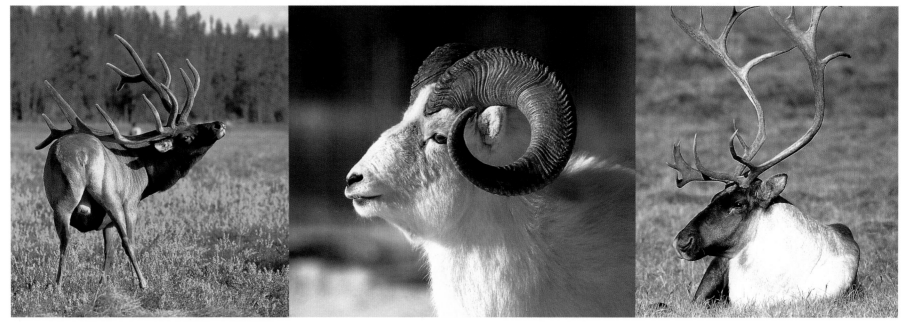

ELK   DALL SHEEP   WOODLAND CARIBOU

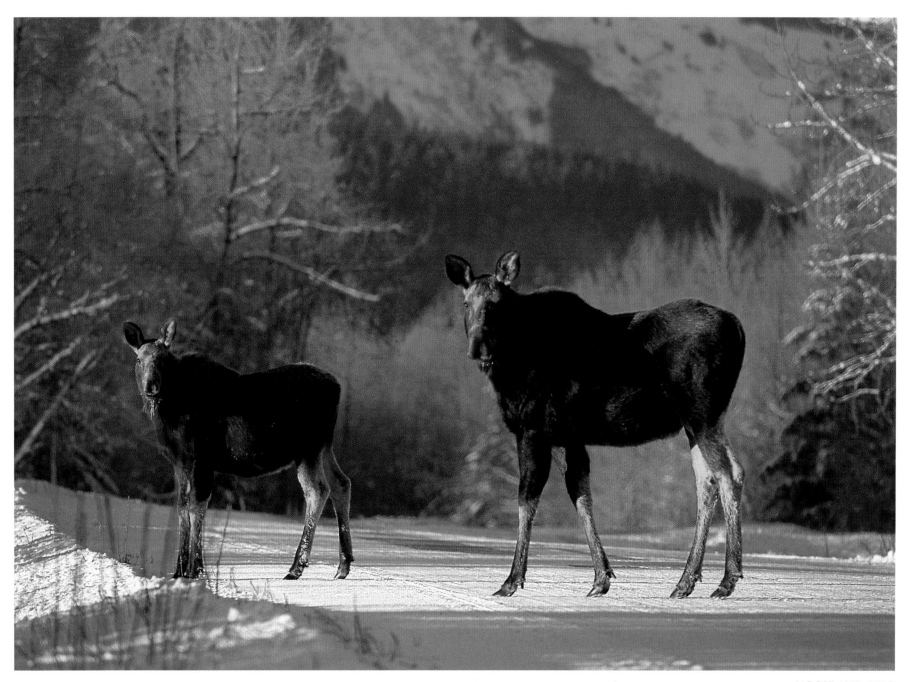

MOOSE AND CALF

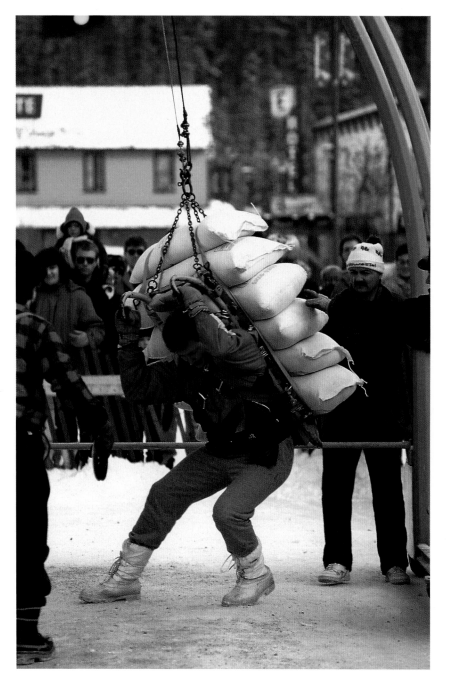

FLOUR PACKING CONTEST AT SOURDOUGH RENDEZVOUS

Winter life

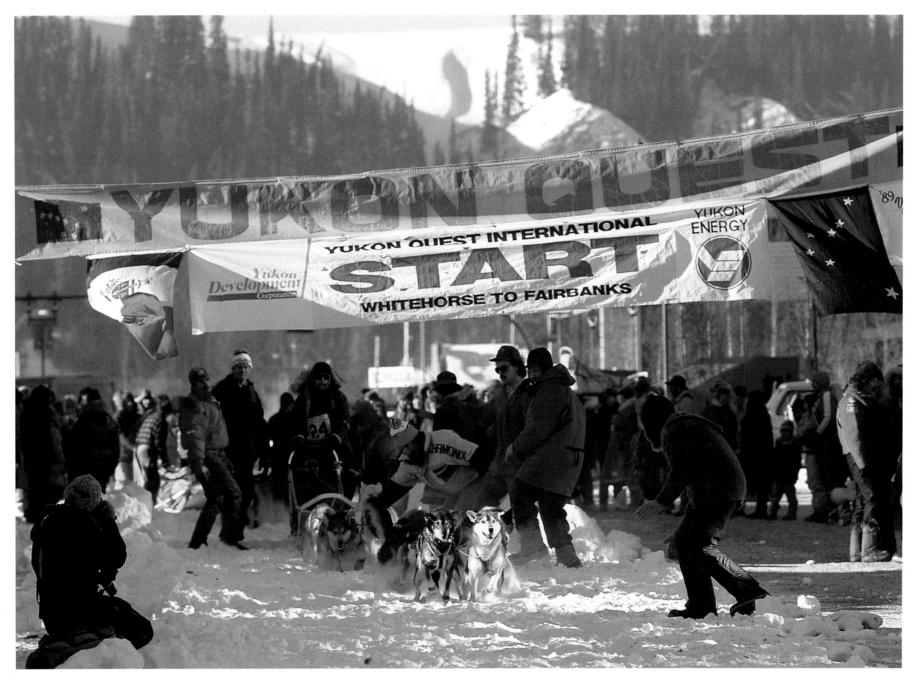

YUKON QUEST START, WHITEHORSE

65

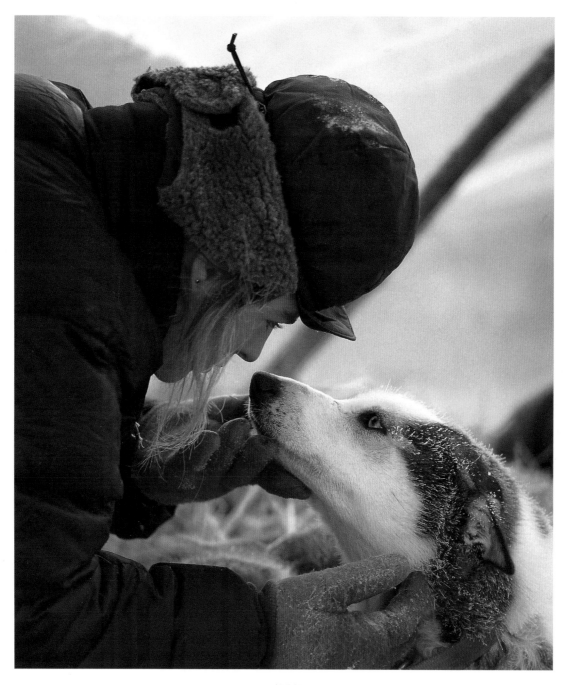

SPECIAL CARE FOR DOGS ALONG THE QUEST TRAIL

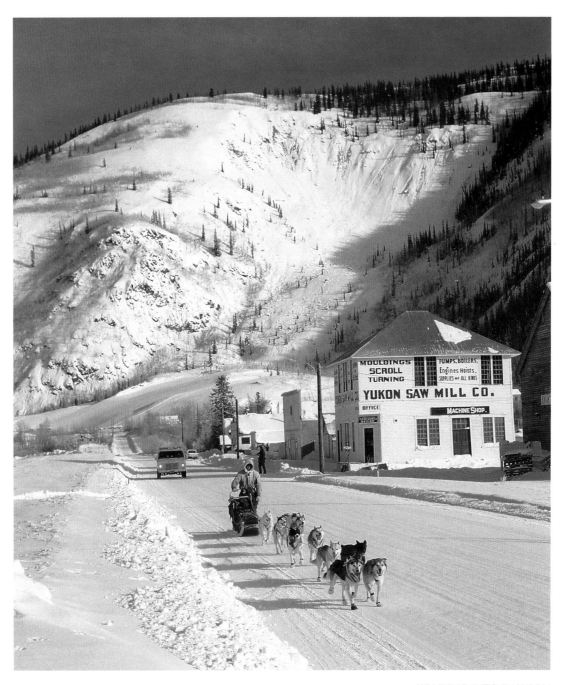

HEADING INTO DAWSON

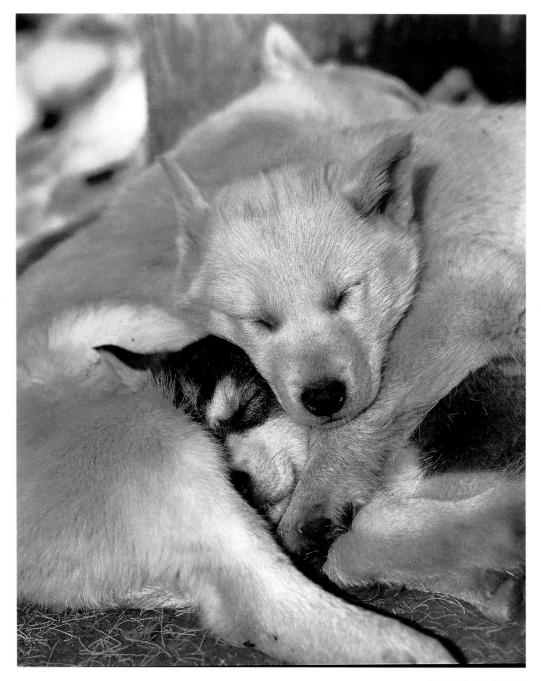

Northern sights

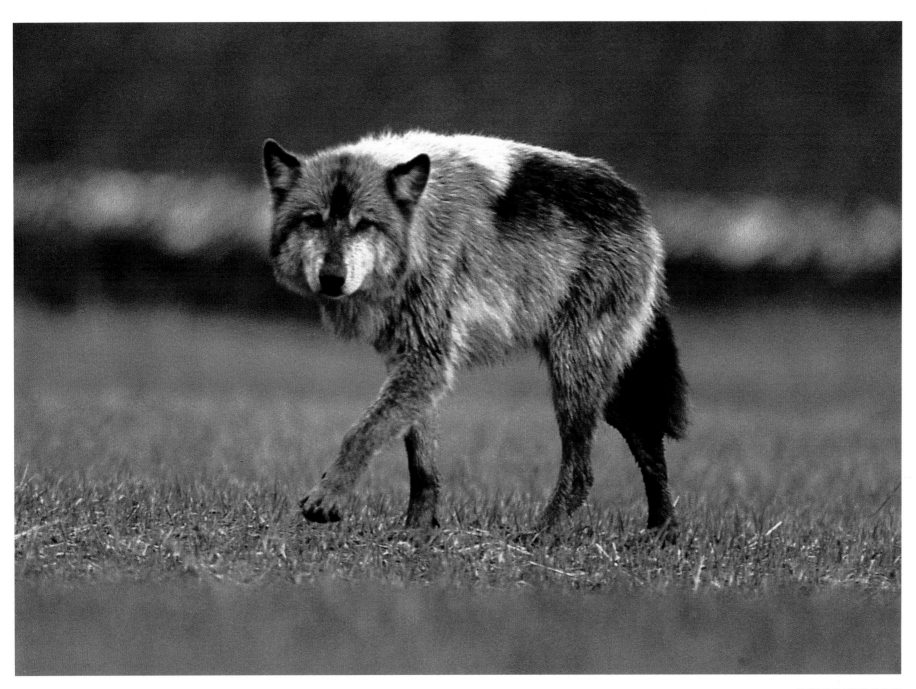

WOLF IN THE WILD

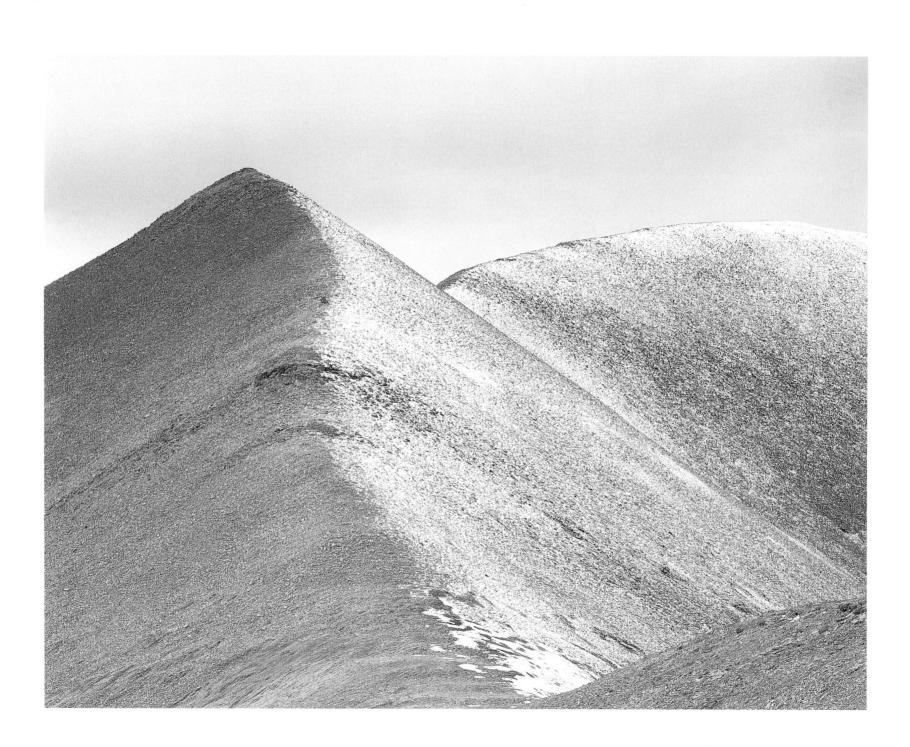

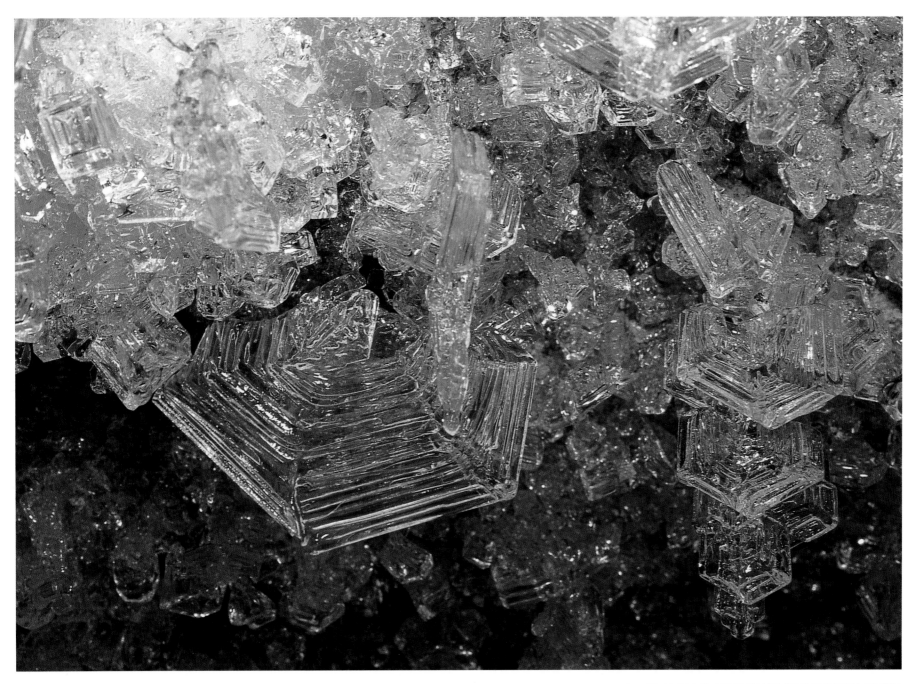

ICE CRYSTALS IN UNDERGROUND MINE SHAFT AT GOLD RUN CREEK

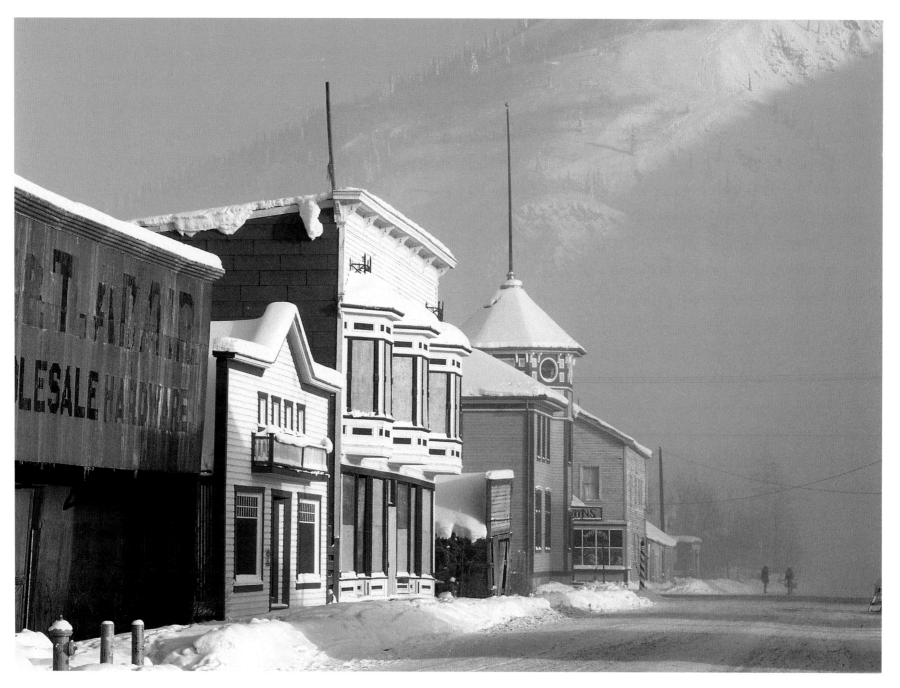

40 BELOW IN DAWSON CITY

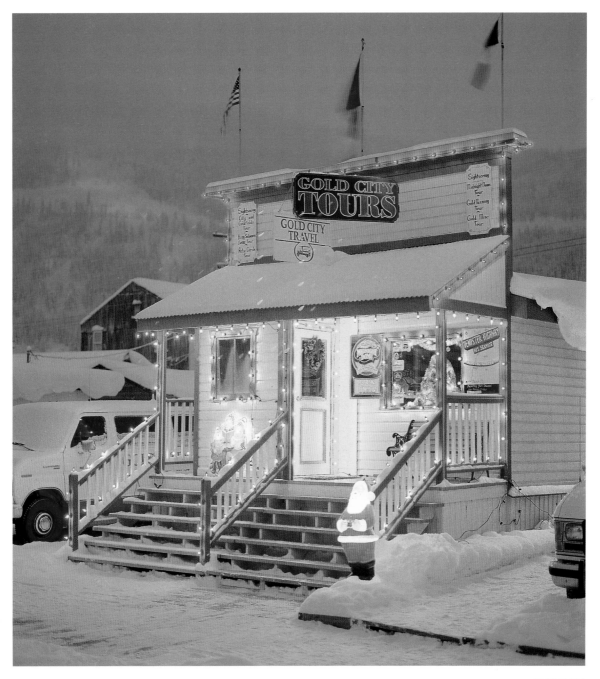

DAWSON

73

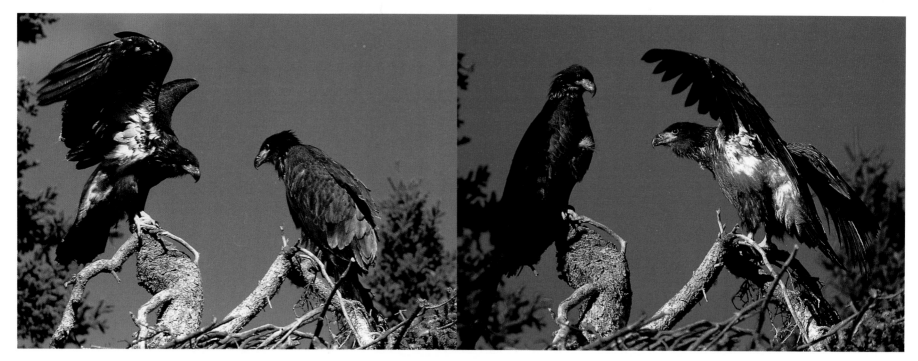

YOUNG EAGLES IN DIALOGUE

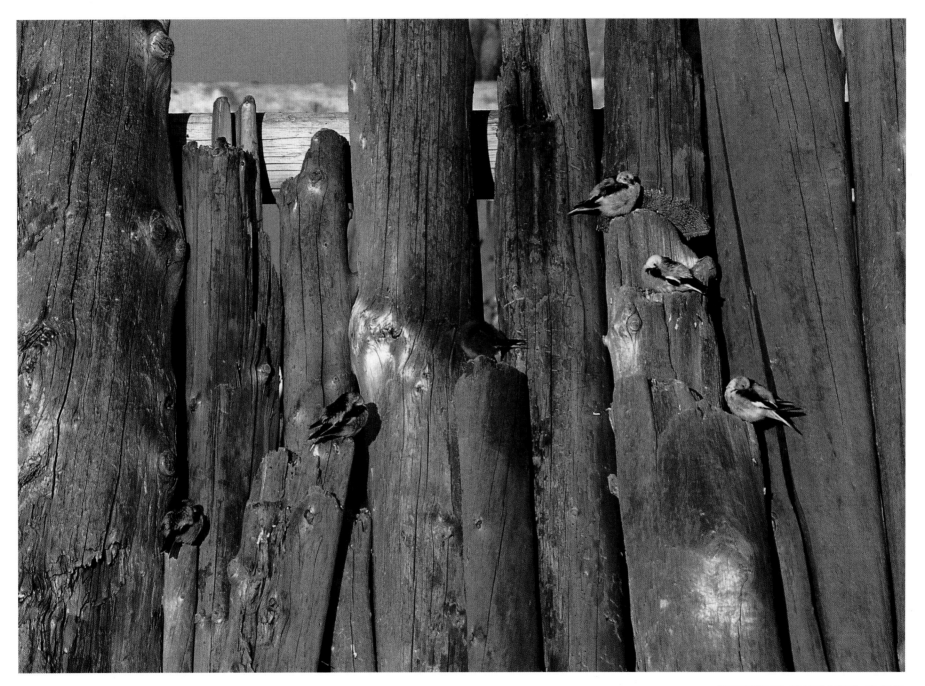

SNOWBIRDS AT HERSCHEL ISLAND

75

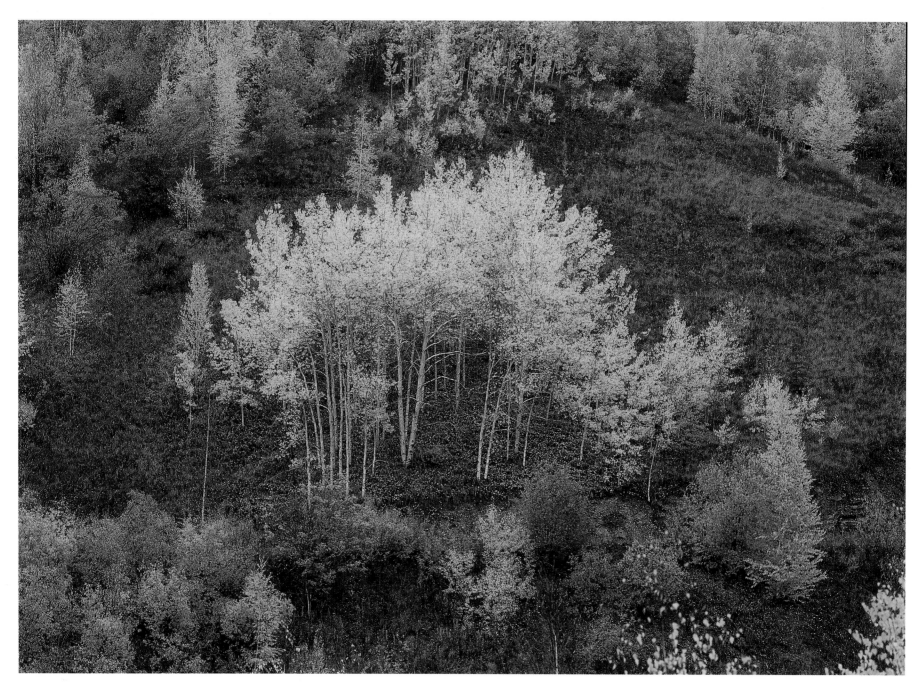

AUTUMN ALONG BONANZA CREEK

Time passing

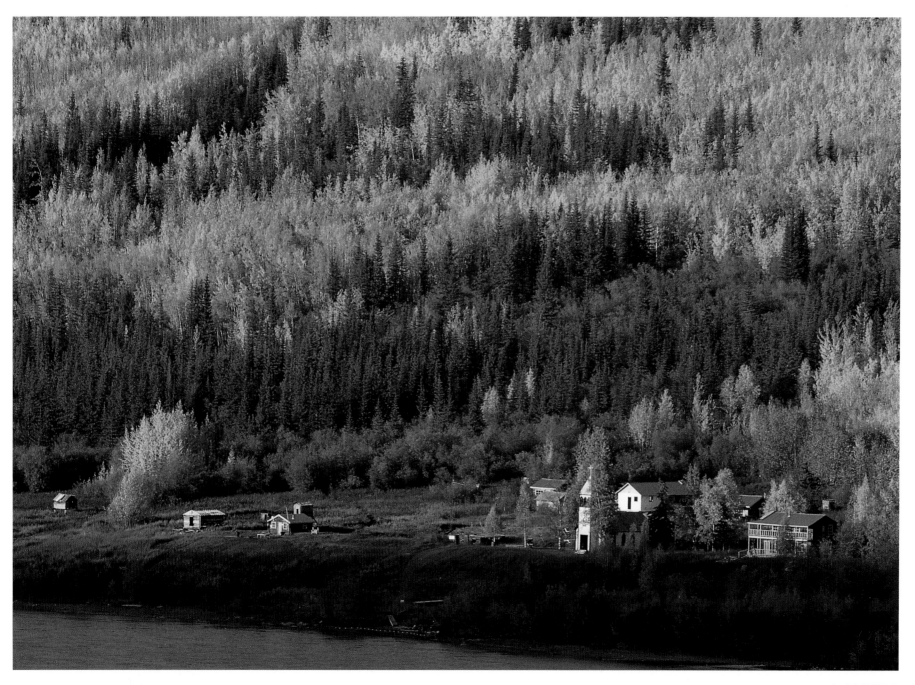

MOOSEHIDE

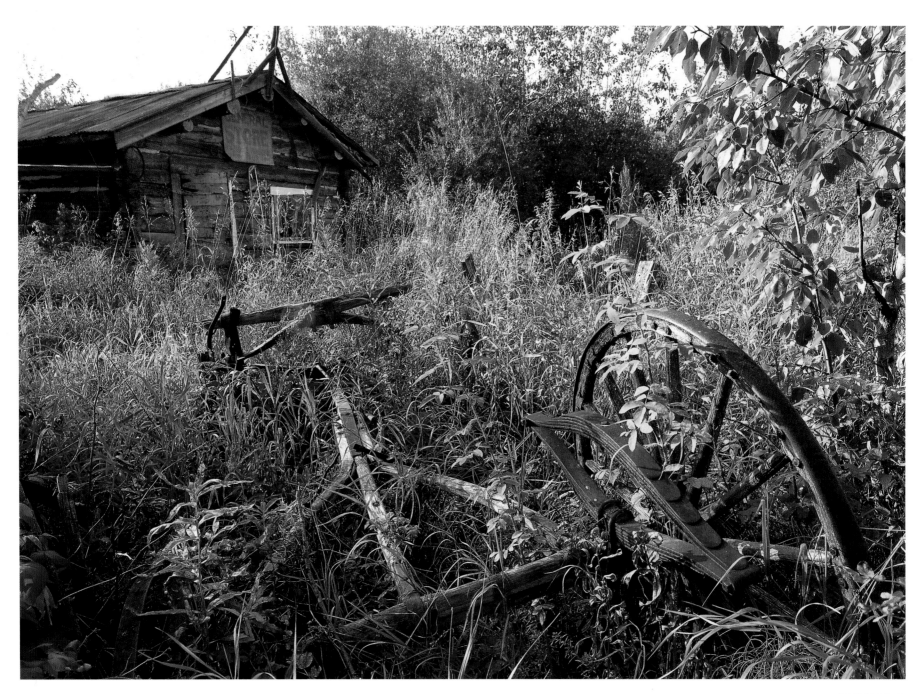

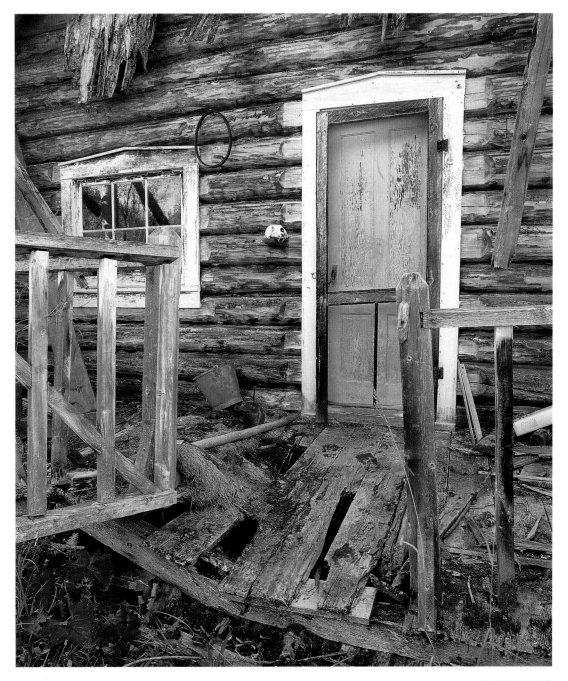

TWELVE MILE

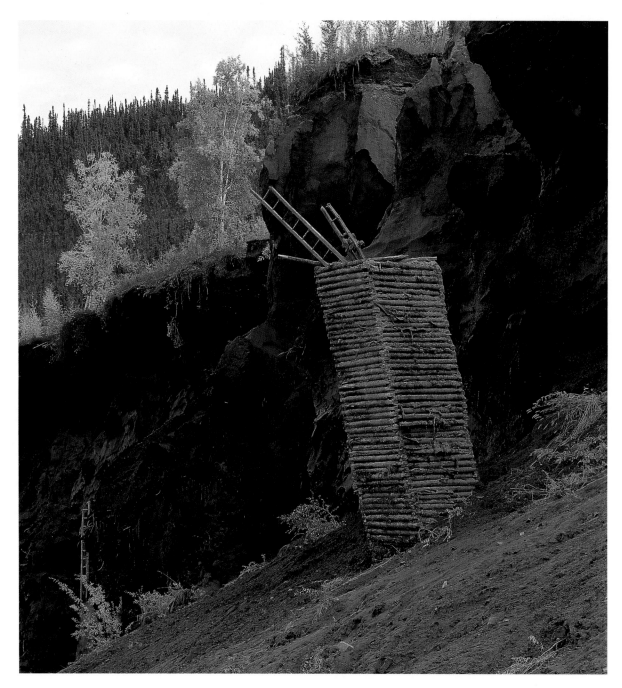

OLD MINE SHAFT UNCOVERED ON HUNKER CREEK

Mining

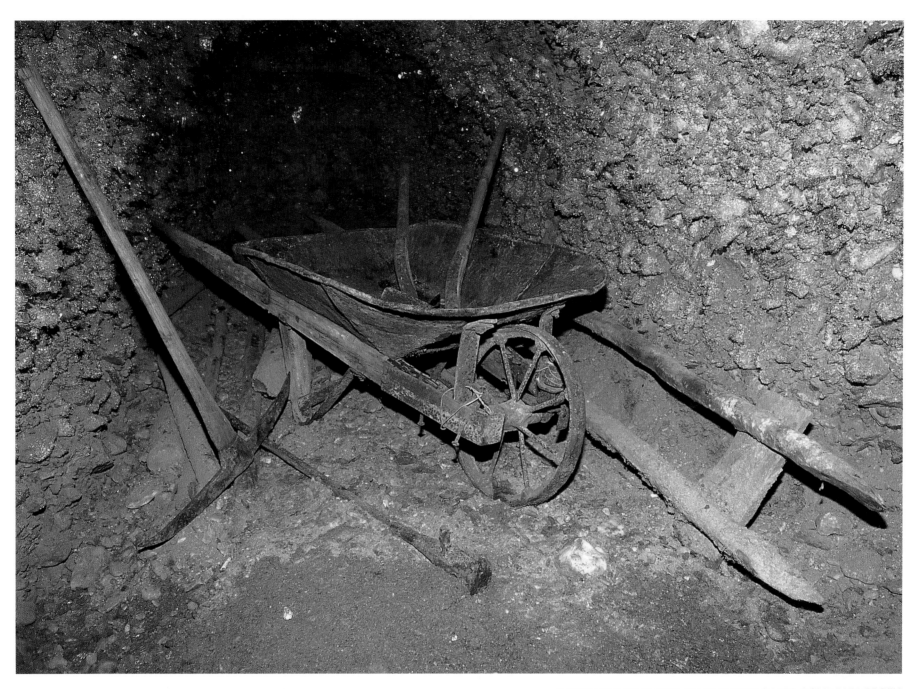

TOOLS LEFT BEHIND IN AN OLD MINE SHAFT, GOLD RUN CREEK

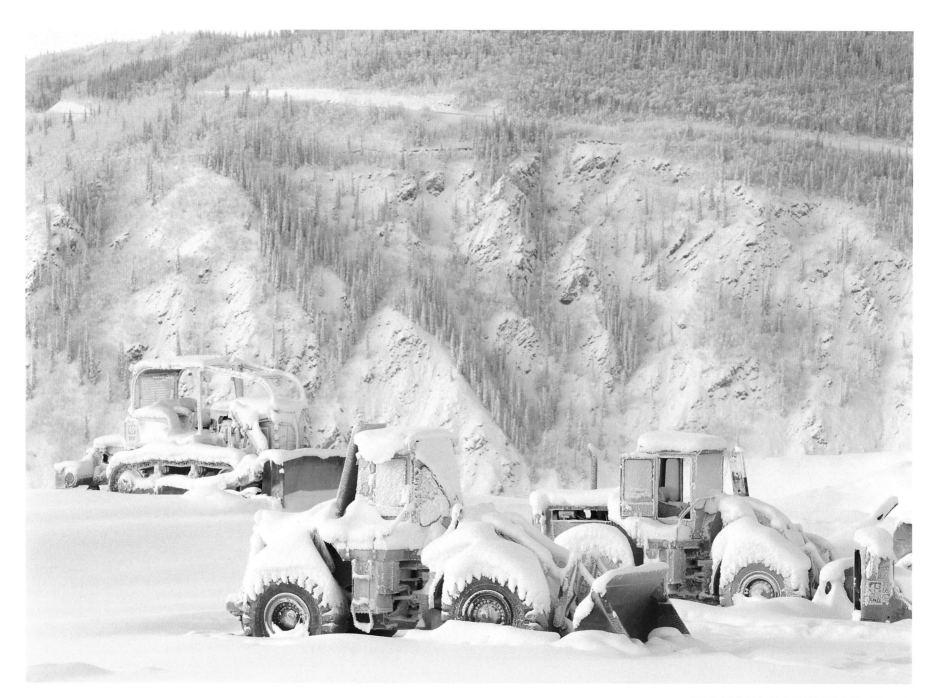

MINING EQUIPMENT WAITS FOR SPRING

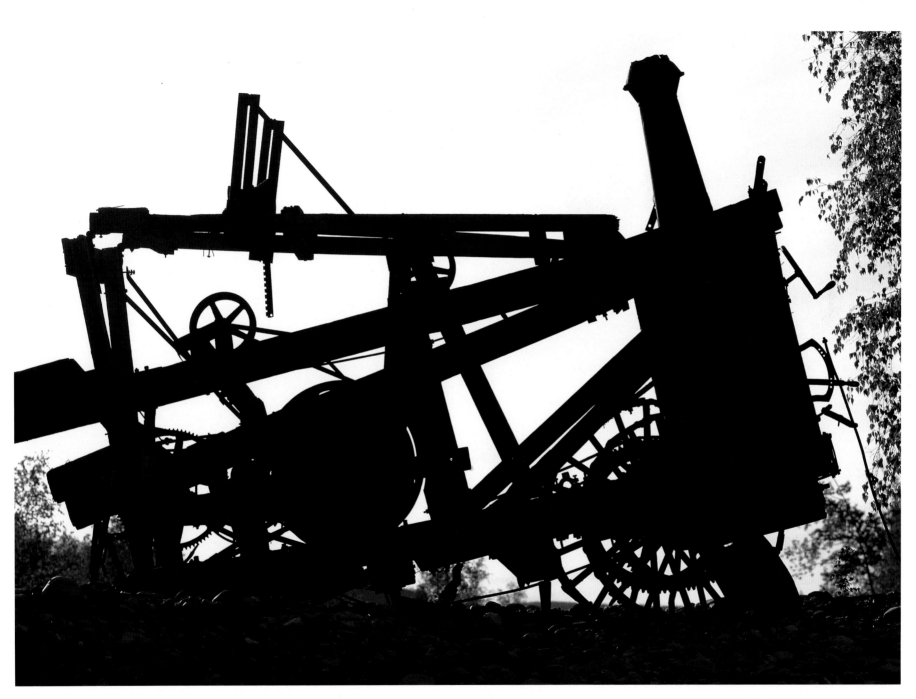

OLD KEYSTONE DRILL, KLONDIKE GOLDFIELDS

83

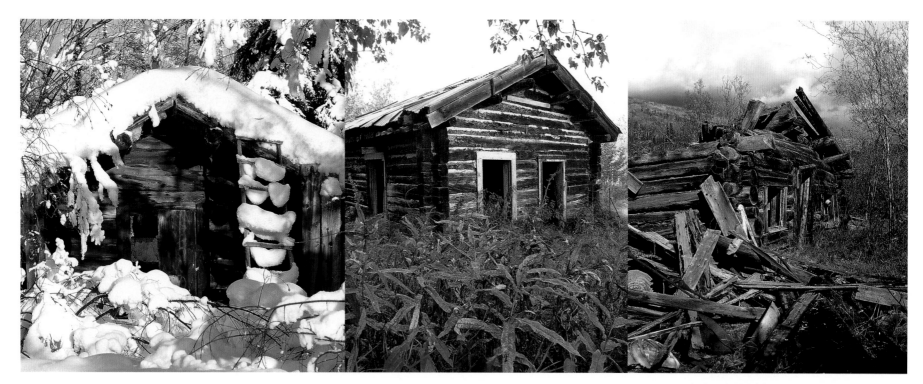

CABINS OF THE KLONDIKE GOLD RUSH

Days gone by

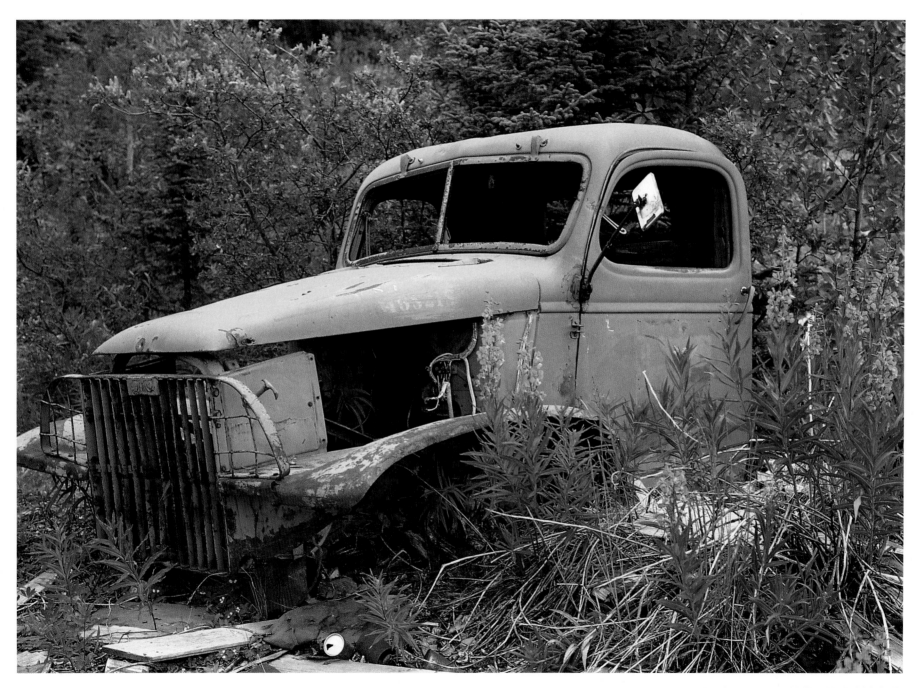

ABANDONED W.W. II VEHICLE, HAINES ROAD

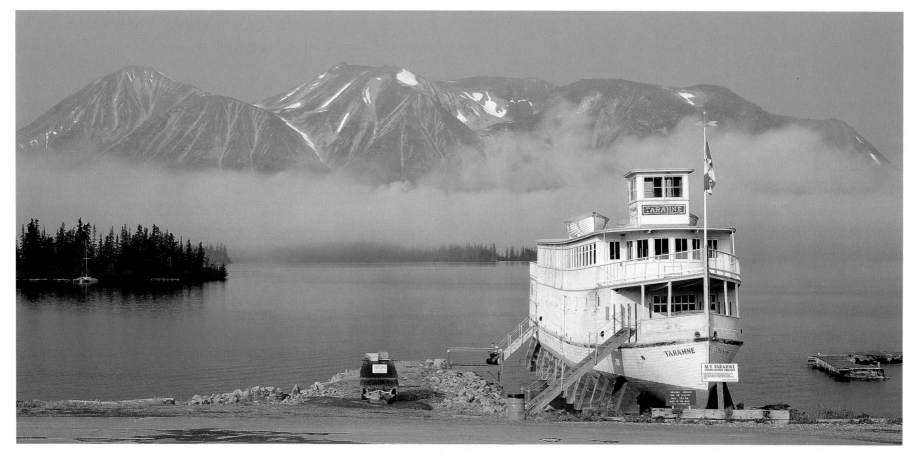

TARAHNE AT ATLIN

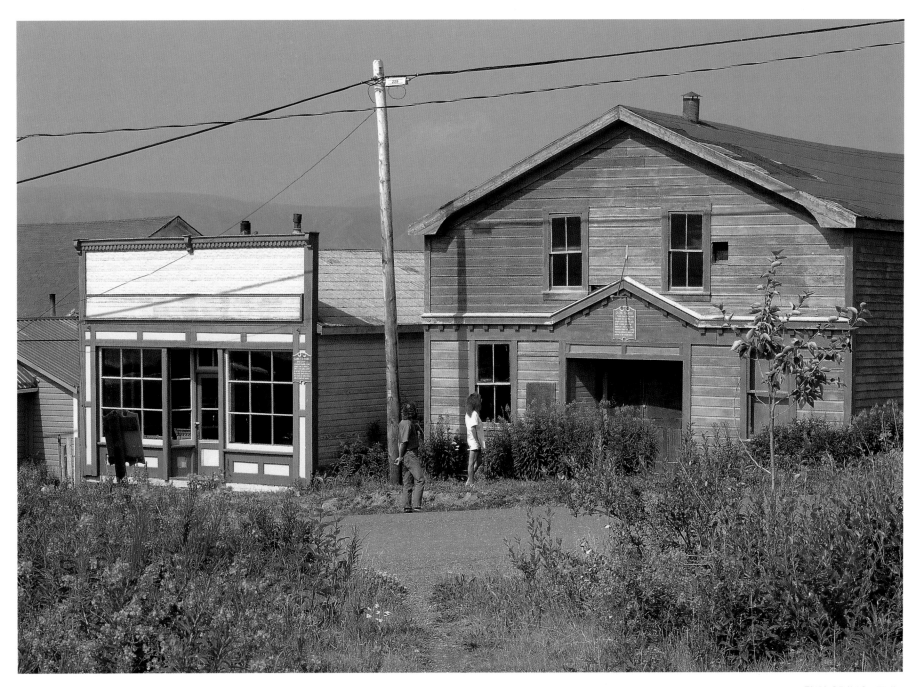

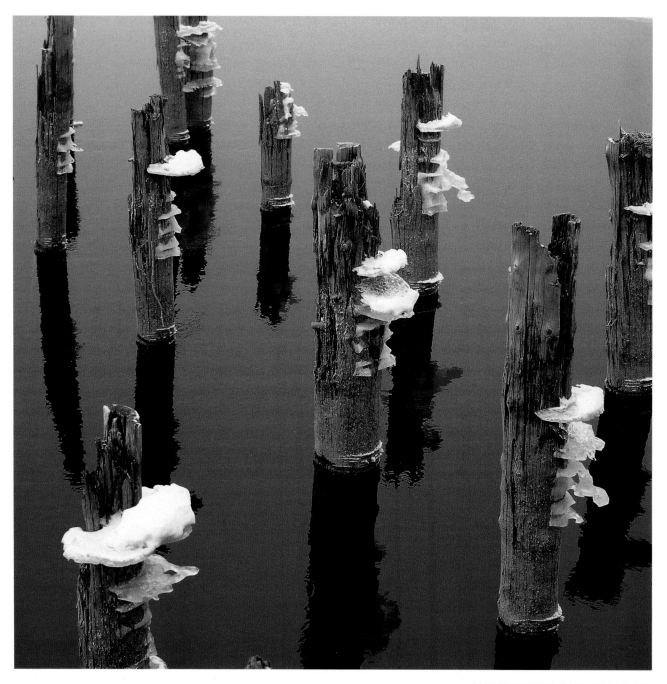

OLD BRIDGE PILINGS, CARCROSS

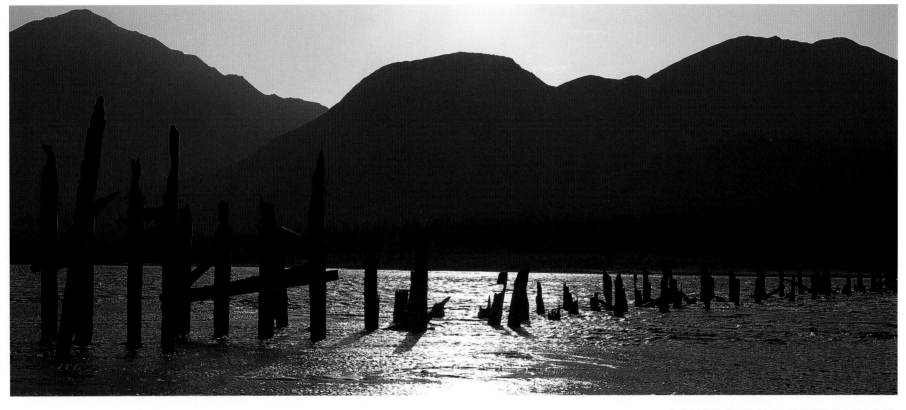

REMAINS OF BRIDGE ON THE SLIMS RIVER

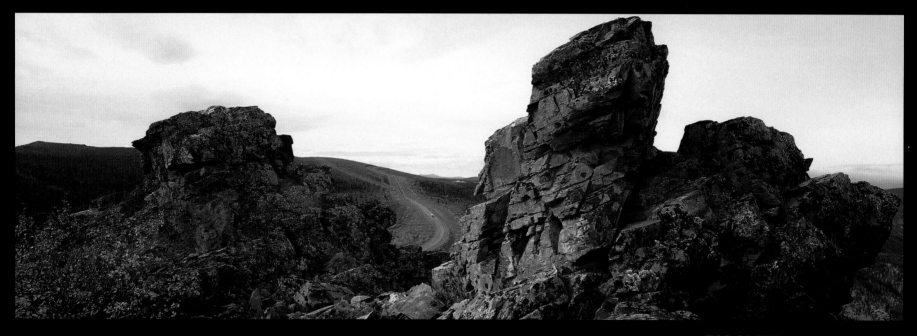

TOP OF THE WORLD HIGHWAY

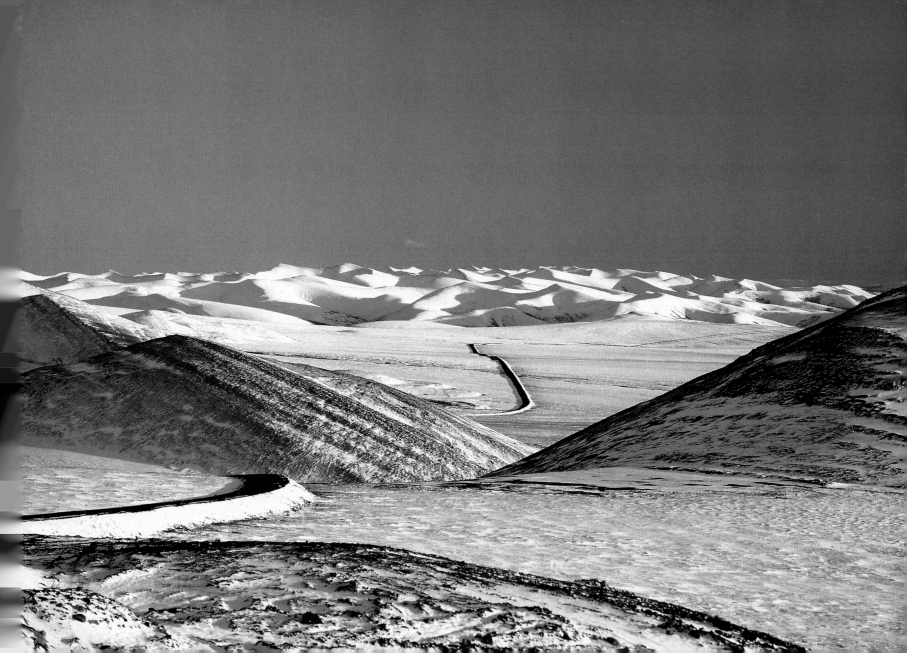

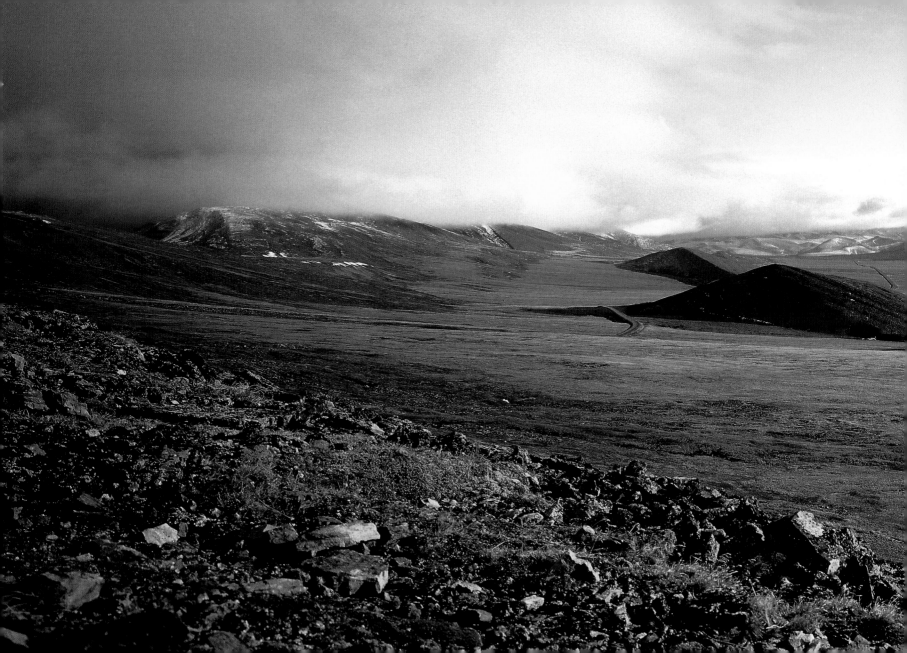

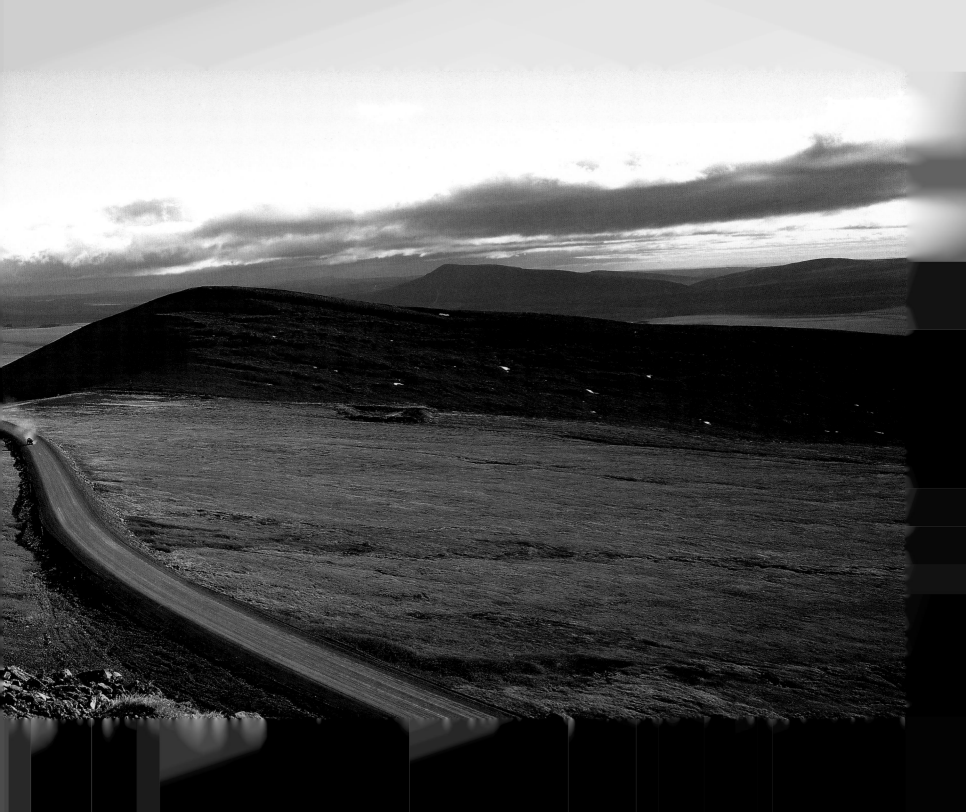

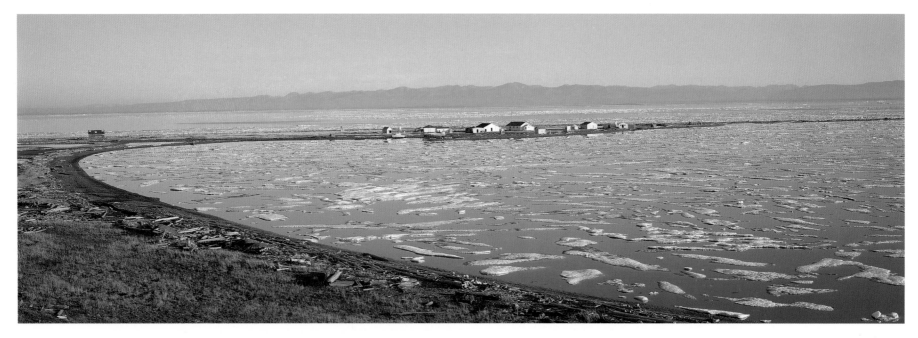

HERSCHEL ISLAND IN JULY, 1 A.M.

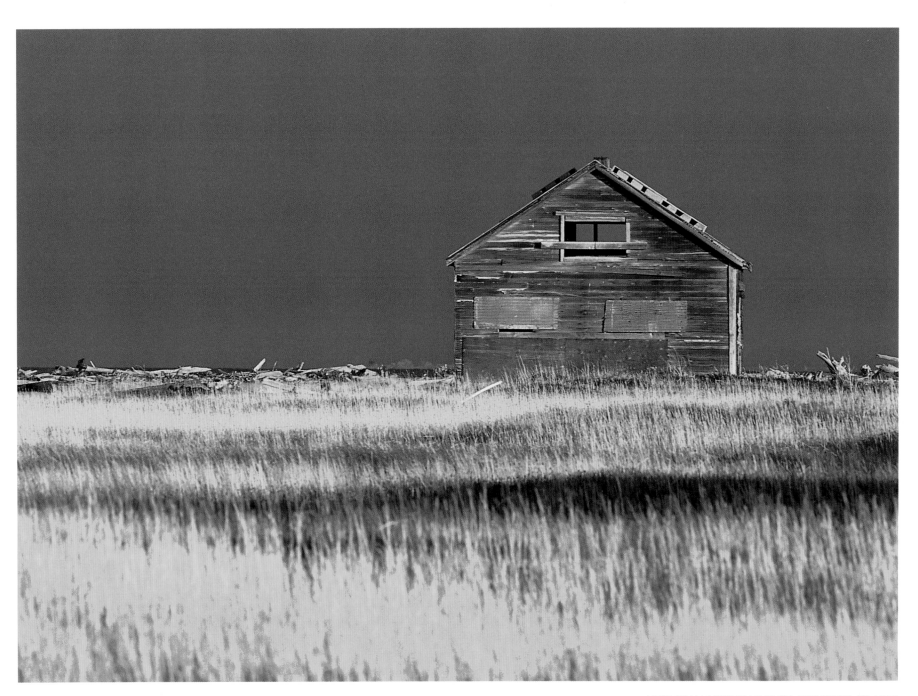

ANGLICAN MISSION HOUSE, HERSCHEL ISLAND

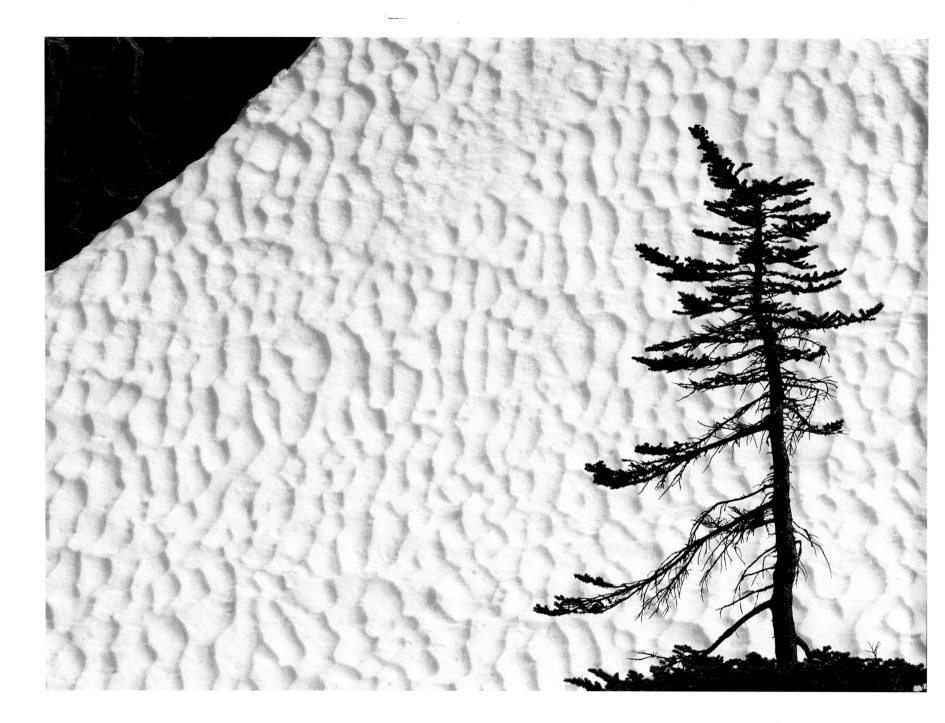

Scenes remembered

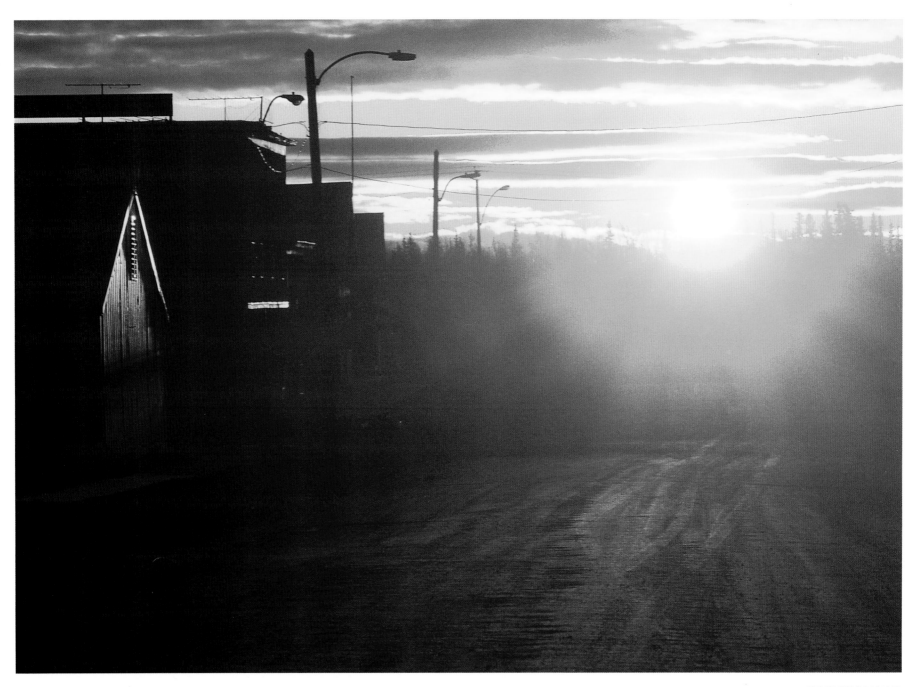

SUNRISE IN MAYO

YUKON HILLS

CARIBOU ENSHROUDED BY FOG ON THE NORTH COAST

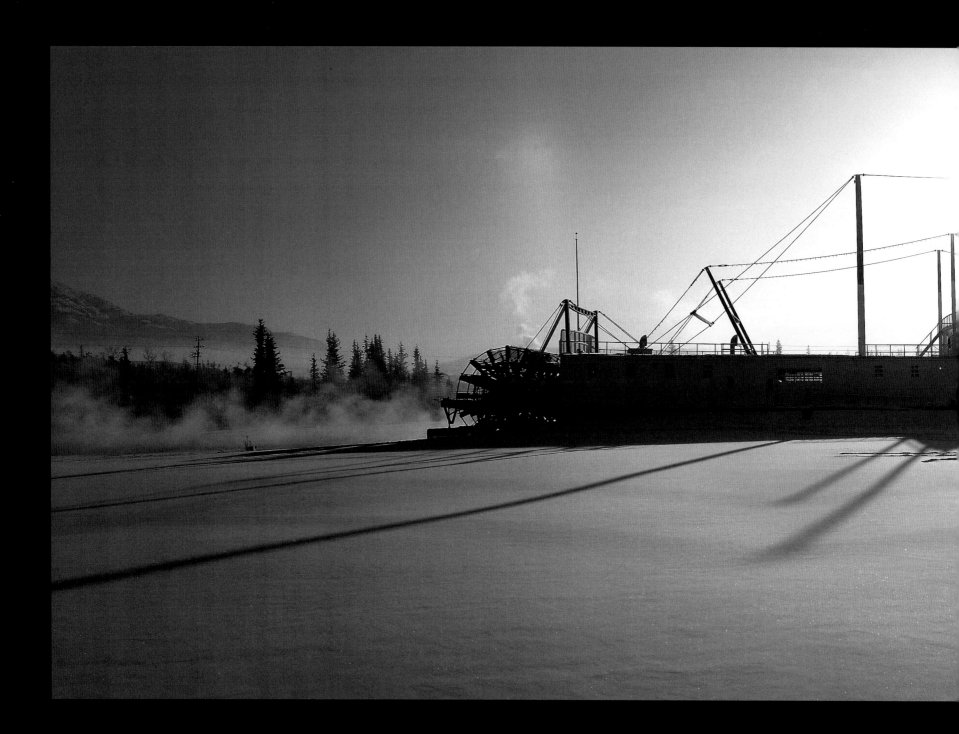

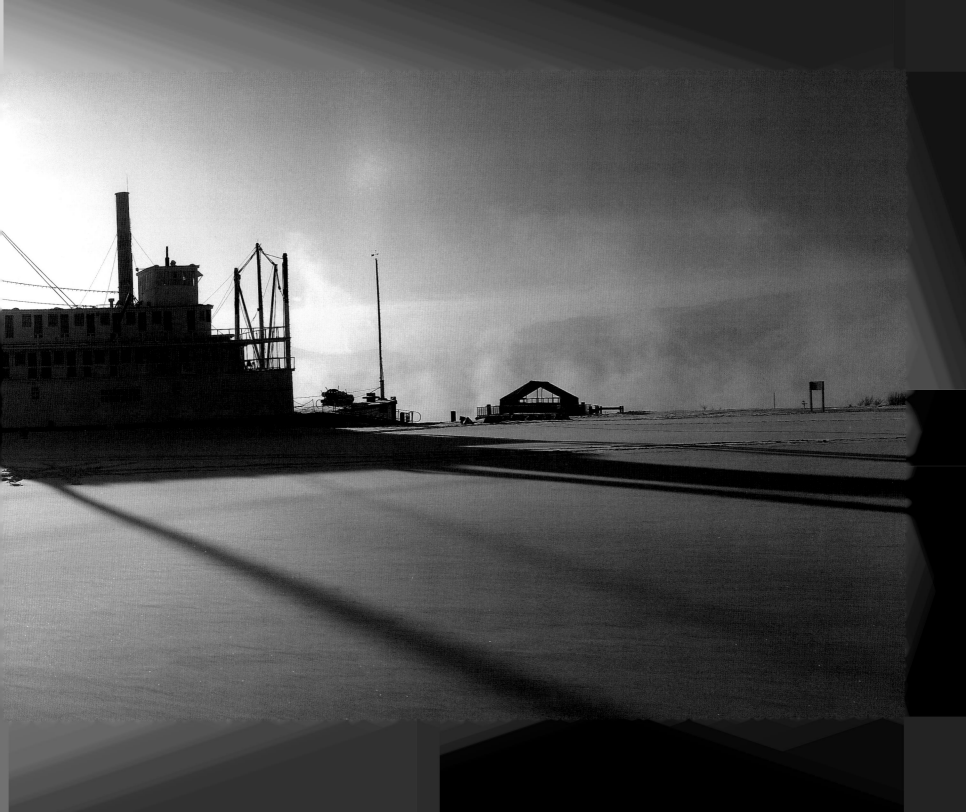

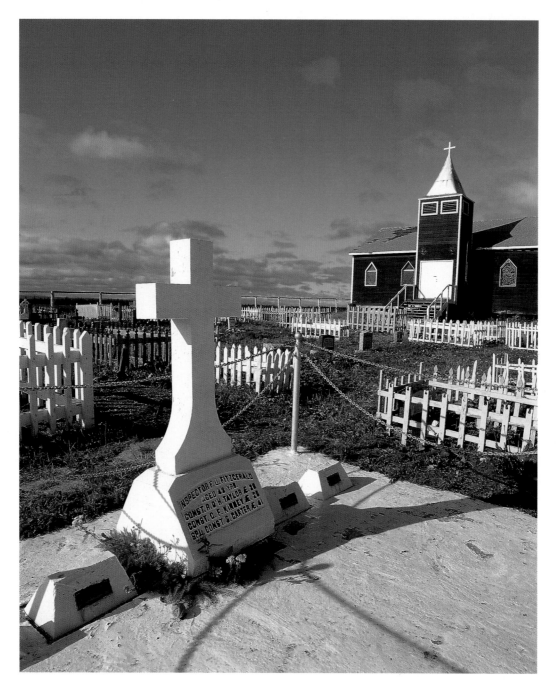

GRAVE OF THE LOST PATROL, FORT McPHERSON

At rest

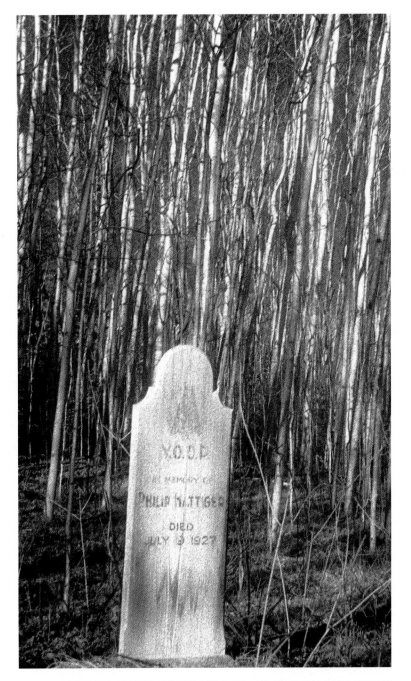

A YUKON ORDER OF PIONEERS GRAVE AT GOLD RUN CREEK

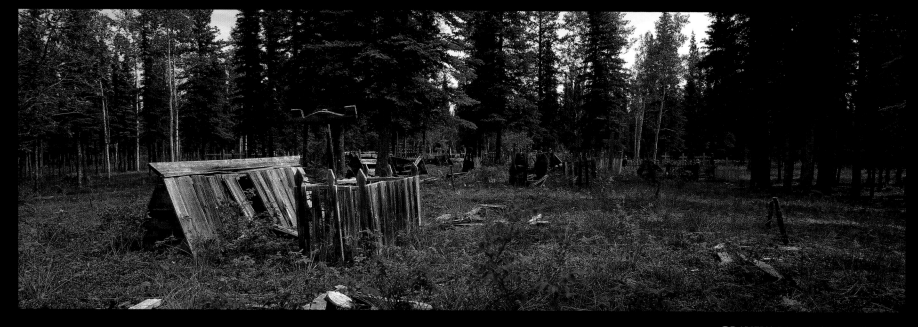

GRAVEYARD AT FORT SELKIRK

104

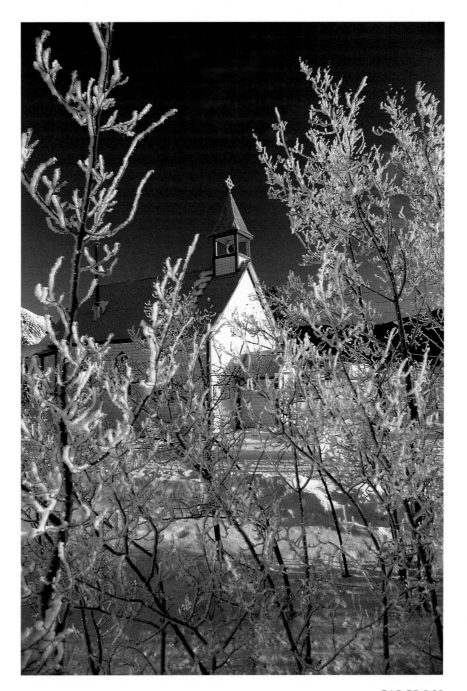

CARCROSS

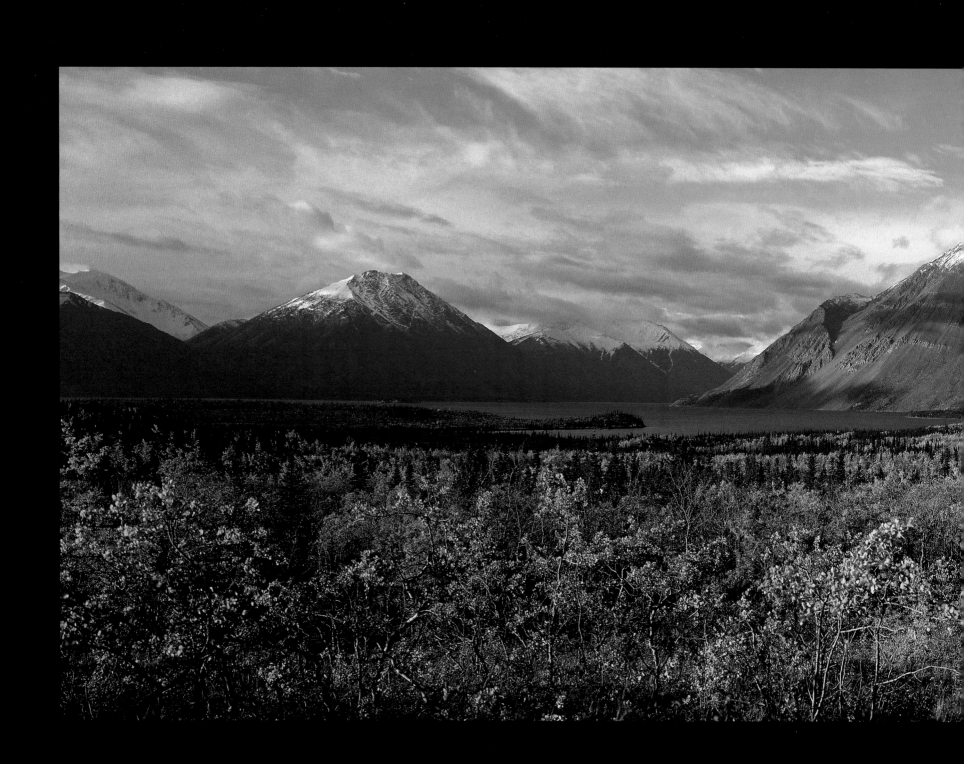

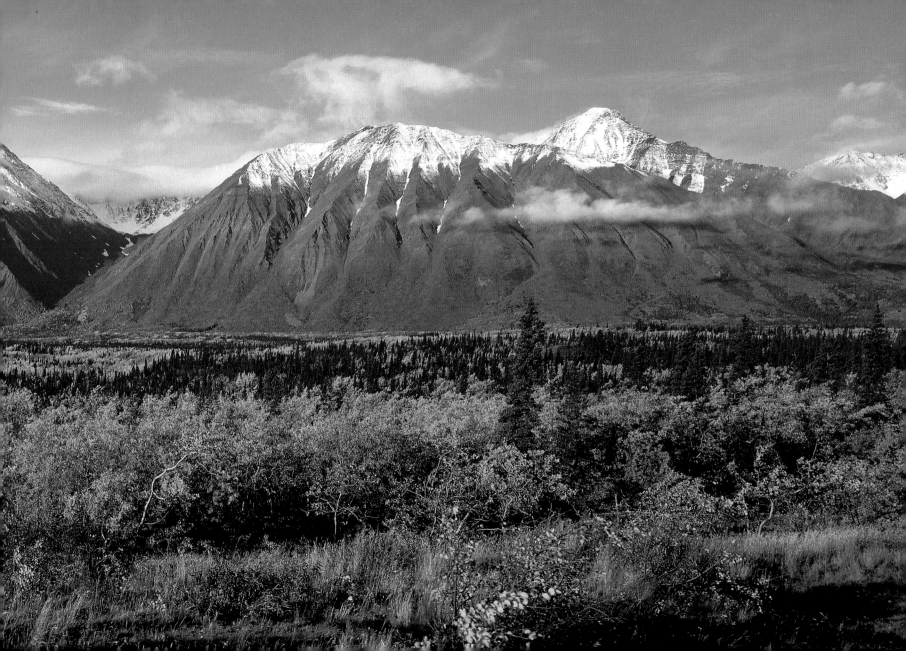

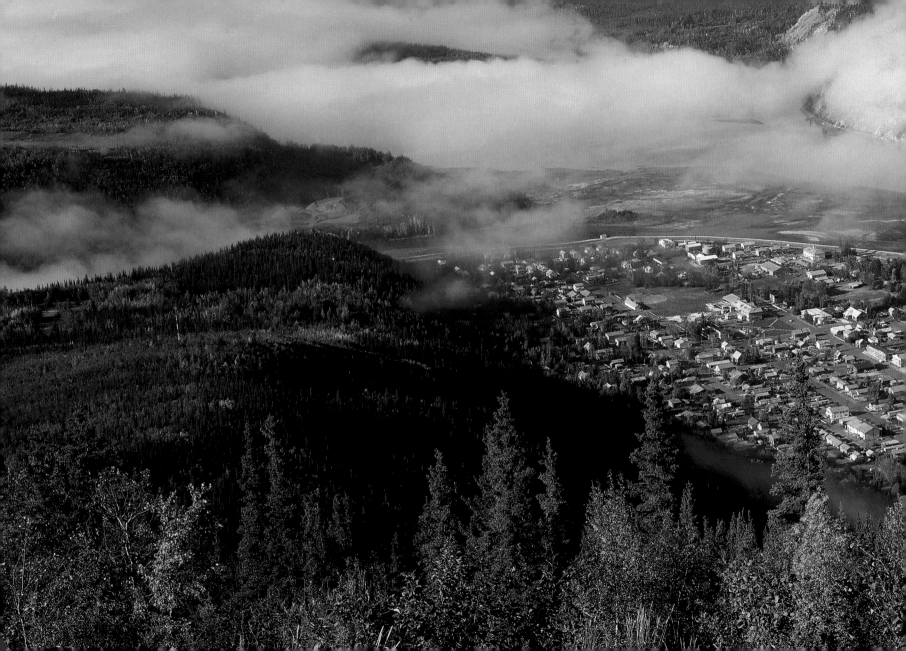

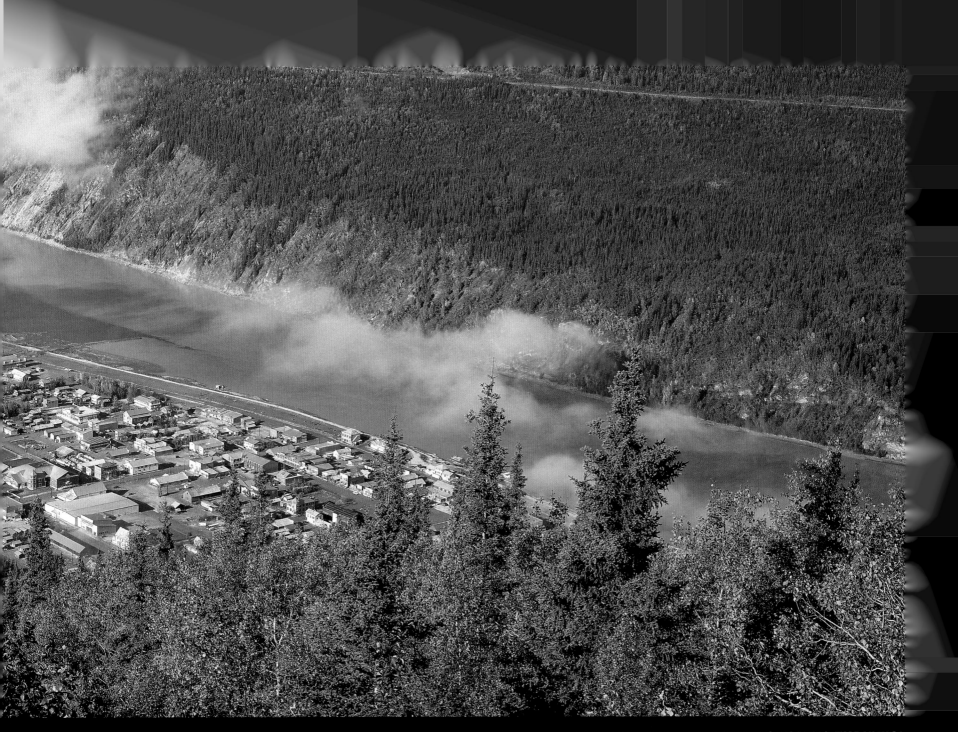

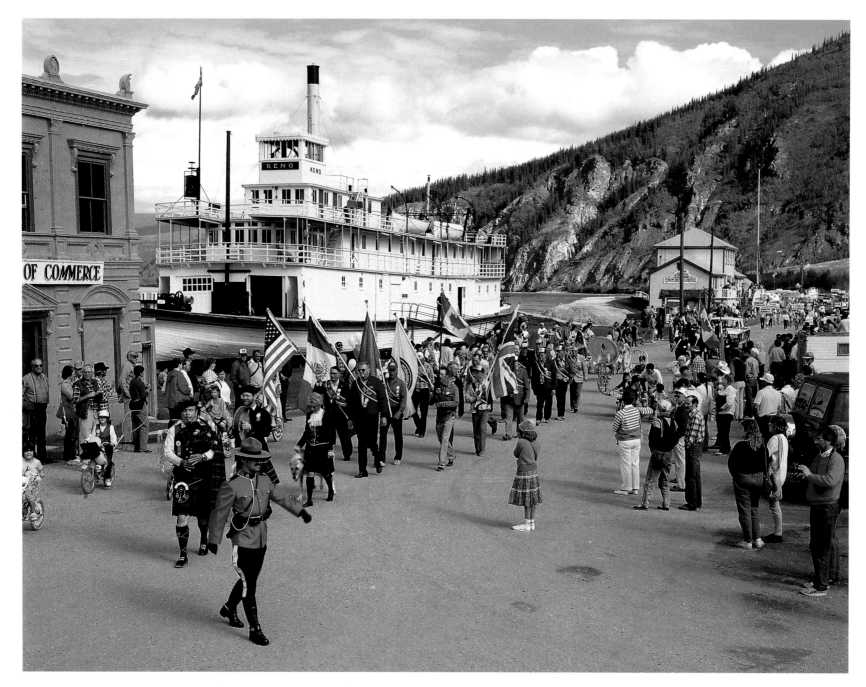

DISCOVERY DAY PARADE, DAWSON

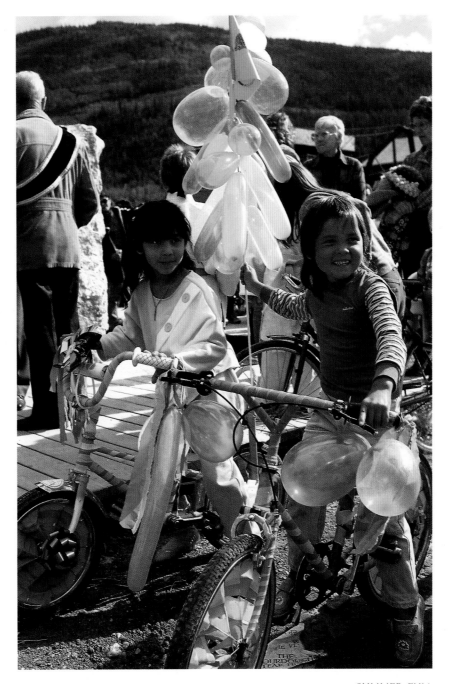

SUMMER FUN

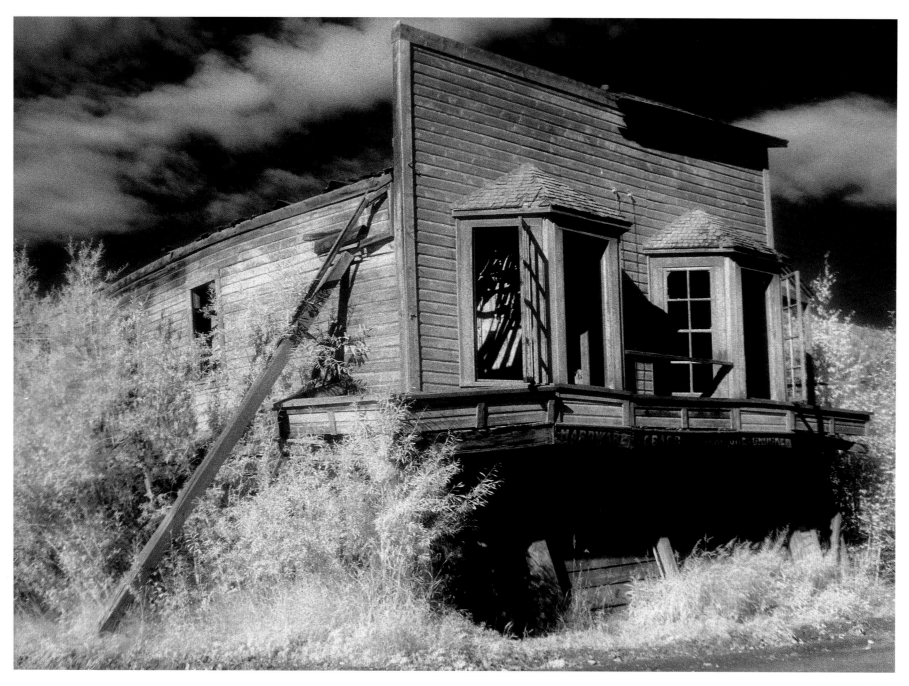

DAWSON CITY

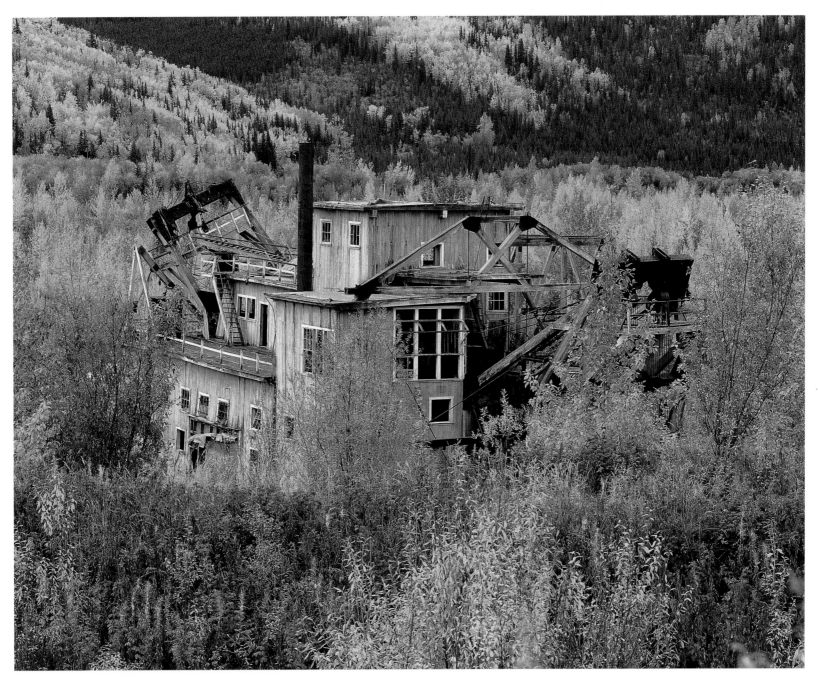

DREDGE AT HUNKER CREEK

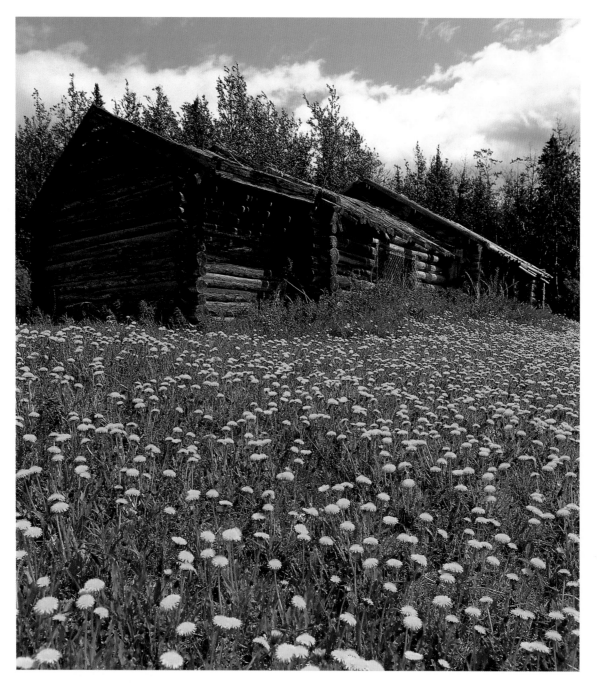

DALTON POST

The Yukon

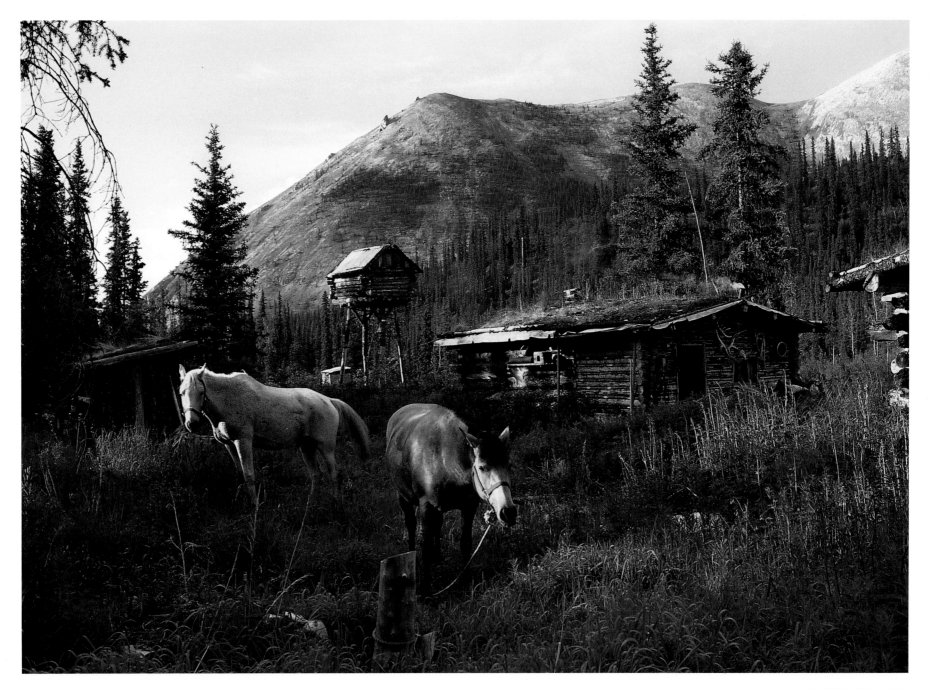

HART RIVER CAMP

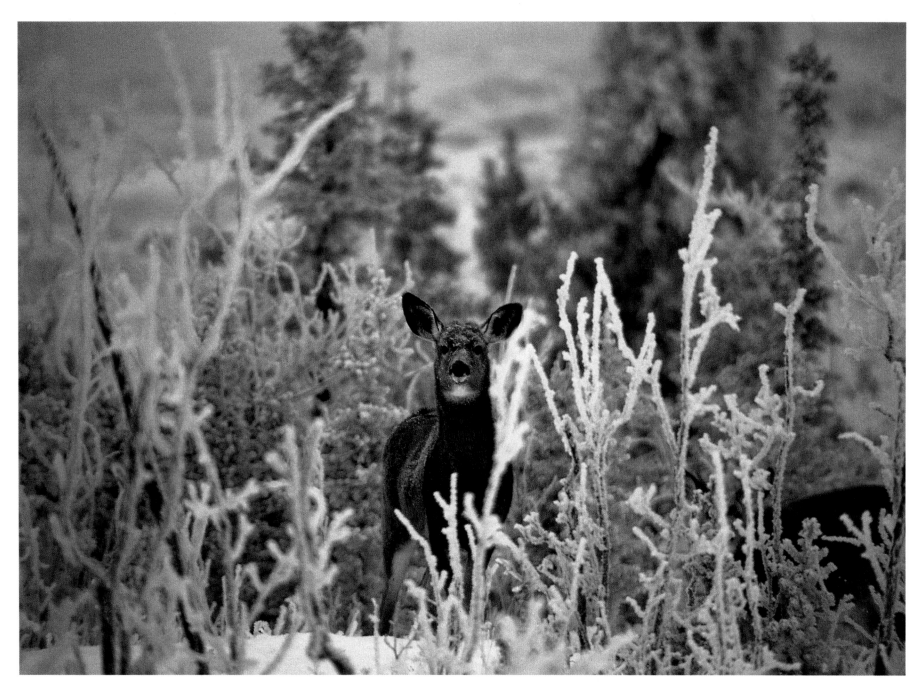

DEER

SUNSET THROUGH FOREST FIRE HAZE

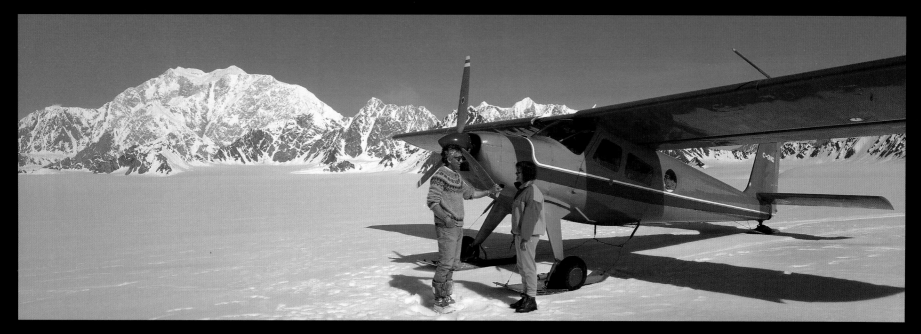

MOUNT LOGAN

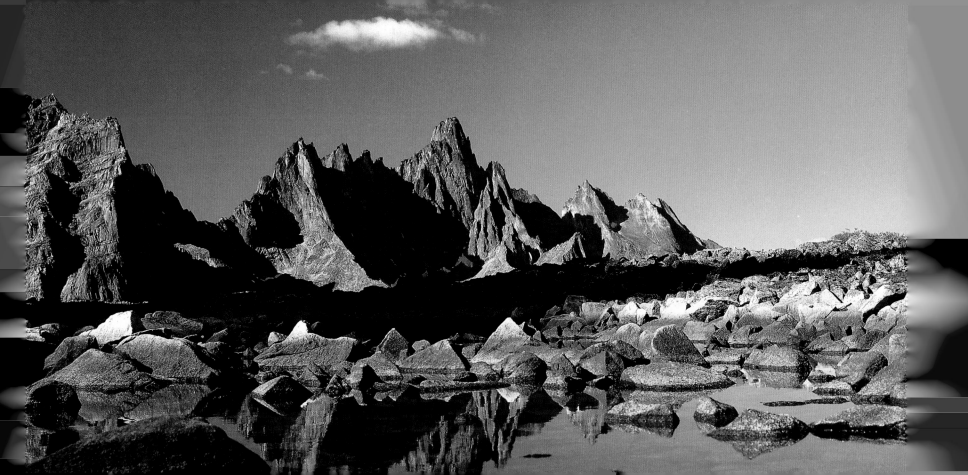

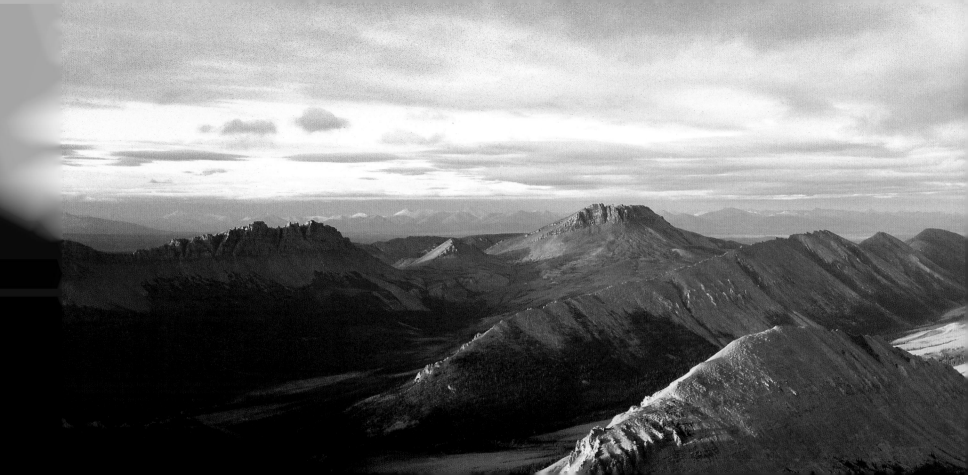

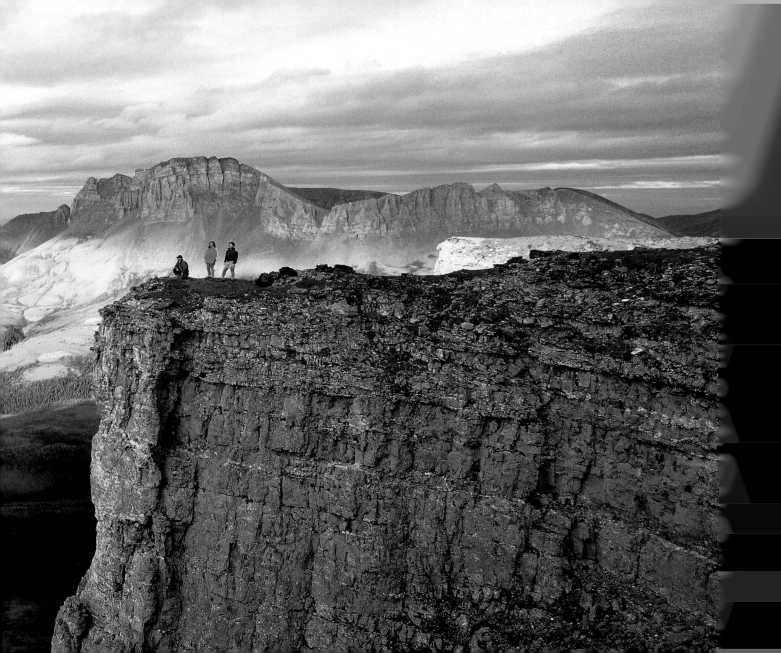

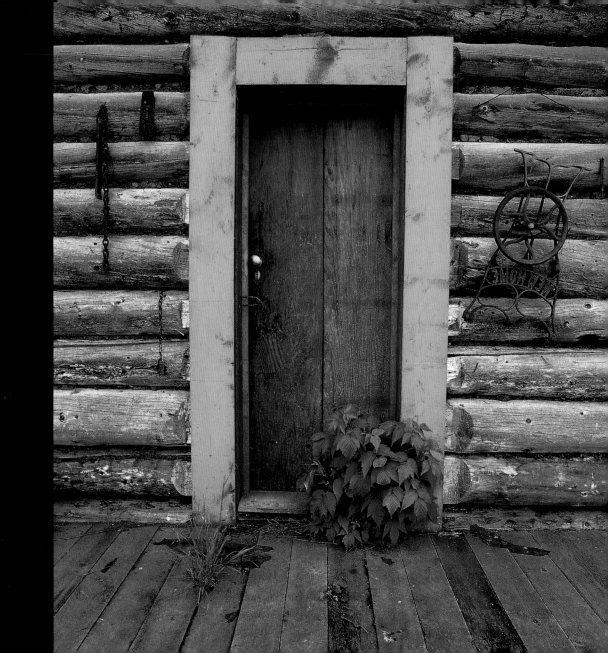